Wow! I Never Knew That!

Wow! I Never Knew That!

12 of the Most Misunderstood and Misused P&C Insurance Coverages, Concepts and Exclusions

Christopher J. Boggs

CPCU, ARM, ALCM, LPCS, AAI, APA, CWCA, CRIS, AINS

Wow! I Never Knew That!

12 of the Most Misunderstood and Misused P&C Insurance Coverages, Concepts and Exclusions

Christopher J. Boggs

CPCU, ARM, ALCM, LPCS, AAI, APA, CWCA, CRIS, AINS

Contents

Chapter 1
Why Do Clients Buy Insurance?

Face it, many insurance practitioners believe there are only two motivations pushing clients to buy insurance: it's a requirement or fear. But insurance professionals know it's because their clients want to get their claims paid at the time of the loss. Let's review each of these reasons.

It's Required

Banks, contracts, and statutes are often seen as an agent's friends. Much coverage is purchased because another entity (or force) is pushing the insurance buying decision. Prime examples of forced insurance purchases include the following.

- Homeowners' coverage is required by the mortgagee.
- Automobile Physical Damage is required by the finance company or lessor.
- Flood coverage is required under federal guidelines before a loan is granted (when applicable).
- Automobile Liability Personal Injury Protection ("No Fault") and sometimes UM and/or UIM are required by statute.
- Workers' Compensation is required by statute or contract.
- General Liability is required by contract.

- ERISA bonds are required by statute.
- Performance Bonds are required by contract.
- Directors & Officers (D&O) coverage is required by corporate documents.

While agents should be thankful that many kinds of insurance are forced purchases, the danger of a required purchase is the misconception that price is (or should be) the deciding factor. GEICO, Allstate, Progressive, State Farm, and others continually (and effectively) play to this mistaken belief as it relates to personal auto coverage in particular.

Even producers fall victim to the idea that the purchase is about price, especially in the early years of their careers. It's amazing how many of us made phone calls that sounded something like: "Hi, Mr. Prospect. My name is Joe Agent, and I'd like to see if I can save you some money on your insurance."

Don't give me that pious, "I have never ..." look. You may never have used those exact words; but have you ever asked to "quote?" It generates the same effect in the client's mind: "Insurance is a commodity, everyone is the same. Evidently price is the best guide for making a decision since I have to buy the coverage anyway."

An agent's duty is to educate the client and explain that not all insurance coverage forms are created equal, even those designed to fulfill insurance purchase requirements. Part of this responsibility is clarifying for the insured that standard forms are designed for the average insured. The problem is, there is no such thing as an average insured. Each insured has individual loss exposures that must be addressed on an individualized basis with endorsements and additional coverages.

Moving the client from buying only the "required" insurance coverage to investing in the "necessary" insurance protection requires tapping into the second reason clients purchase insurance- fear. Don't misunderstand; this use of the term fear does not constitute the knee-knocking, butterflies-in-your-stomach type of fear. Respect may be a better term. It is respect for what could happen and the financial consequences of the undesired event.

Fear/Respect

Fear or respect for the possibilities and realities of an injury or loss occurring is exampled when clients purchase higher liability coverage than the minimum limits required by statute. The possibility of major financial hardship is also why clients continue to purchase a homeowners' or a commercial property policy long after the mortgage debt is paid.

Other examples of client fear broadening the insurance buying decision include, the following (not an all-encompassing list).

- Umbrella/Excess Coverage (although it may be required by contract in some commercial situations)
- Life Insurance
- Personal Articles Floaters or Inland Marine Coverage (may be subject to contract)
- Crime Coverage

- Employment Practices Liability
- Equipment Breakdown (Boiler & Machinery)
- Business Income Coverage

None of these is required by law, although some may be subject to a contract. So why do clients purchase these and other such voluntary coverages? Fear of the consequences of a loss. Essentially, clients want to be able to sleep at night; insurance protection can allow some rest. (I won't say peace as that does not come from insurance or anything external.)

How is such fear/respect created? Agents who know policy language, how to identify coverage gaps, how to conduct exposure analysis, and how to fix gaps in protection create the necessary respect for loss possibilities.

Lest you misconstrue my point, this is not fear mongering. It is telling clients the truth about their situation. Agents who fail to point out the client's exposures, coverage gaps, and remedies for those exposures and gaps are doing a huge disservice to their clients (and creating an errors and omissions exposure for themselves). The agent's responsibility is to create some fear, some discomfort in their clients so they can make an informed decision about coverage.

Clients must be allowed to make the insurance-buying decision with all the necessary information. If some of that information creates discomfort or fear on their part that is not a bad thing. The other end of the spectrum is the insured who thinks everything is just fine because the agent was the one who was afraid; afraid to provide all the pertinent information.

This is the insured who makes the buying decision based on price and who is very upset when he has a claim for an uncovered loss.

Don't be afraid of the client saying, "You're just trying to sell me more insurance." No, you're not, and a proper response might be, "No, I just want you to know the realities of your situation. Protecting yourself against the financial consequences of what could happen is a business decision. Please initial here that we discussed this exposure."

It takes guts to be an insurance professional. First, you have to become proficient in policy language. Then you have to be willing to use that information to help your clients make buying decisions. Even if they don't purchase the protection, you have done all you could. It's nothing personal. It's just a business decision for the client. And if they refuse and have an uncovered loss, you've done all you could. Go home and sleep well.

Don't be afraid of fear in the insurance buying process. The information that creates this fear allows an informed business decision. But, above all, be honest about the realities.

Really Only One Reason

Regardless of any other supposed reason, such as requirement or fear, clients really buy insurance protection for one reason only: to get claims paid at the time of a loss. Although they don't necessarily know or verbalize this need, this really is the only reason insurance is purchased. The agent's job is to make sure that need is satisfied by knowing policy language, understanding the breadth of coverage, and knowing how to cover any gaps in protection.

Why This Book

This book is dedicated to coverage knowledge. As the title of the book suggests, this is a guide through 12 of the most misunderstood or misapplied coverages or exclusions. Also provided is bonus information in the form of three chapters highlighting endorsements agents should actively seek and those that should be avoided.

True insurance professionals look for and search for information that can help them stand out from the crowd of "also rans" in the insurance industry. Not all insurance practitioners are created equal; some are more committed than others. This book is for those who are committed to being the best.

Chapter 2
CGL Coverage for "Intentional Acts"

Intentional acts are not excluded by the commercial general liability (CGL) policy. Exclusion 2.a. deletes only "Expected or Intended Injury," not an expected or intended act. An injury is the result of an act, and only if the result is expected or intended, can the claim be excluded.

In support of this conclusion the meaning of the word accident, as used within the definition of occurrence, refers to the outcome, not the action leading to the outcome. If this were not the case, very few instances of bodily injury or property damage would ever be covered by the CGL.

Combine the legal definition of accident with the expected or intended injury exclusion and the intended breadth of the CGL's protection is clear. In application, if the intentional action was expected to or intended to cause injury or damage, only then is such injury or damage not considered an accident and subject to the exclusion. Any approach to general liability coverage that applies a different view of the use of this exclusion/definition combination, as its logical conclusion, requires that the original action (act) itself be accidental before coverage applies.

As an example, consider a drywall subcontractor that misses the stud and instead drills a drywall screw into a water pipe. Six months after completing the job, the screw rusts away, resulting in massive amounts of water damage. Is this a covered completed operations property damage claim under the CGL?

Yes! Even though drilling in the screw was intentional, hitting the water pipe was accidental. The result of the intentional act is accidental damage which is covered by the policy. If the policy was not viewed and applied this way, the drywall contractor, in essence, would have had to accidentally drill the screw into the wall for coverage to apply, not just accidently drill it into the water pipe. Coverage would, in effect, be non-existent.

The difference is expectation and intent. The subcontractor intended to drill into the stud but missed. This is an intentional act with an unexpected/unintended result. If, however, the drywall subcontractor drilled the screw into the water pipe on purpose following an argument with the general contractor, he obviously expects and intends some level of damage, and any subsequent damage is excluded. The subcontractor intentionally drilled in a screw with the same result in both instances (water damage), but with differing original intents.

Misapplication of the Exclusion

Some insurance company claims adjusters apparently operate under the mistaken belief that the CGL includes an intentional acts exclusion. A recent incident relayed to me from a professional friend evidenced this.

A pressure washing subcontractor was cleaning the exterior of a newly completed house. Following the cleaning process, the general contractor (GC) discovered that the chemicals used by the pressure washer severely damaged and destroyed the appearance of several layers of bricks on one part of the house (not the entire house, just one part). The GC, of course, turned in a claim against the pressure washer requesting to have the bricks replaced.

The pressure washer's insurance carrier denied the claim stating that the damage was the result of an intentional act (pressure washing the bricks with cleaning chemicals) and thus not accidental. The pressure washer was, understandably, livid. His question was the same as mine. If the carrier isn't going to pay for damage caused by pressure washing because it's an intentional act, why have the coverage (other than to satisfy a contract requirement)? No claim would ever be paid if such an extreme interpretation is allowed.

The chemicals applied were used for the purpose for which they were designed and the means of application were per instructions and industry standard. The pressure washer intended to clean the exterior of the house, but he did not intend the damage that ultimately resulted. Had the pressure washer used a chemical known to cause damage to bricks or knowingly acted in some manner such that injury or damage would or should be reasonably expected or intended, the denial would have been reasonable.

What Is Excluded?

One court stated, "An intentional act exclusion precludes coverage only if the insured acts with specific intent to cause bodily harm or if the facts demonstrate that harm is substantially certain to result." Two key phrases jump out: specific intent and substantially certain. A Florida court said, "We explained that an 'occurrence,' which is defined as an 'accident,' encompasses damage that is 'neither expected nor intended from the standpoint of the insured.'"

Notice also that the phrase within the exclusion, from the standpoint of the insured, negates the reasonable and prudent test often applied to questions of negligence. The insured must reasonably expect or intend injury or damage for the exclusion to apply. This wording does not allow for any attempt to assert what someone else thinks is reasonable or was intended; only what the insured reasonably expected or intended.

Absent the insured's specific intent to cause injury or damage or the substantial certainty that injury or damage will result, the unintended result of the insured's actions meets the classic definition of an accident and is covered by the CGL. Remember, intentional injury or damage is excluded by the CGL; not an intentional act.

Continued Debate

Keep in mind, actions can be intentional yet result in unintended injury or damage; such claims are covered by the CGL. Only when the injury or damage (result) is intended or expected does it no longer qualify as an occurrence or accident. Non-occurrences and non-accidents are excluded by the CGL.

Several insurance-focused groups on LinkedIn have hosted interesting coverage debates. One debate involved an "auto-booting" company that placed a boot on the wrong vehicle. The vehicle owner (an attorney) sued the company for loss of use of the vehicle. The insurance carrier denied the claim on the basis that there was no property damage. Well, the definition of property damage includes the loss of use of undamaged property; so that attempted denial is incorrect.

Several individuals partaking in this online debate asserted and held tightly to the idea that even though the loss met the policy definition of property damage, there is still no coverage because the insured's act was intentional, not accidental. The problem with this argument, as has been detailed in this chapter, is that there is no exclusion for an intentional action, only for an expected or intentional injury.

If the insured (the auto-booting company) knew it was the wrong car and placed the boot out of spite, the resulting loss of use *is* intended from the standpoint of the insured. Once it moves away from a true accident to an intended injury or damage, coverage is excluded. But until it moves from unintentional to intentional, there is still coverage.

Based on the facts of the case as they were presented in the forum, the insured did not know it was the wrong car and was not being malicious in placing the boot. This was an intentional act with unintended injury.

However, the exclusion uses the conjunction "or" (expected or intended). "Or" is an exclusive term meaning that if either of the conditions exists, there is no coverage (or there is coverage if that is what the particular section is intended to accomplish). Although the injury was not intended, the insured should reasonably expect that the owner of any car with one of its boots in place would lose the use of the vehicle.

Because the loss of use is expected by the insured, there may be no coverage available even though the target of the boot was unintentional. In effect, booting the wrong car is a business risk to which the boot placement company is exposed; and insurance provided by the CGL is not generally intended to cover a business risk. Their business is to boot vehicles; if they boot the wrong one, that's a risk they take. Damaging a vehicle is a different story; the insured is not in the business of causing actual property damage.

Coverage is likely unavailable in this case, but not because of the intentional act. The loss will likely be excluded because of ability to foresee the loss of use inherent in the nature of the business.

Conclusion

When evaluating the CGL's expected or intended injury exclusion in light of the entire policy (including the definition of "occurrence" and the legal definition of accident), remember it is expectancy or intention that triggers the exclusion, not the act. Does the insured intend to cause injury to a particular person or entity? Should the insured reasonably expect his actions to cause injury or damage to another party? If the answer to both is "no," then coverage exists.

Key Questions

- Did the insured intend to cause bodily injury or property damage?
- Should the insured have reasonably expected his actions to cause bodily injury or property damage?

Chapter 3

Understanding the Absolute
Pollution Exclusion

Never let it be said that an insurance carrier would grasp at any possible means to deny a claim; but the absolute pollution exclusion is likely the most misapplied exclusion within the CGL policy. Reasons for improper denials by application of the pollution exclusion are varied, ranging from the claim adjuster's misunderstanding of the true proximate cause of the injury or damage to a complete lack of understanding regarding the exclusion itself. Courts, too, contribute to misapplication because of inconsistent rulings among jurisdictions.

Insurance Services Office's (ISO's) unendorsed commercial general liability policy contains what is historically referred to as the absolute pollution exclusion (APE). Although called an "absolute" exclusion, it is far from absolutely excluding all pollution-related injury or damage.

In fact, a close reading of exclusion 2.f. reveals five self-limiting factors, exceptions or requirements within the exclusionary wording.

1. **"Arising out of..."** Before the exclusion can apply, a causal connection must exist between the release (etc.) of the supposed pollutant and the bodily injury

or property damage. The presence of pollution does not and should not automatically trigger the use of the exclusion.

2. **The substance must be considered a pollutant.** States do not apply a universal definition of pollutant. Each applies its own judicial opinion regarding what constitutes a pollutant. Some jurisdictions are very narrow in their definition, limiting the definition of pollutant to substances subject to federal environmental laws. Other states define the term very broadly (sometimes ridiculously so).

3. **There must be release of pollutants.** Within the exclusion is a list of possible ways the pollutants can be released. It can be discharged, dispersed, seep, migrate, or escape. At issue within this self-limiting factor is how the subject jurisdiction defines a release. Some states consider it a term of art and limit the definition of release to the definition found in environmental laws (the laws that the original editions of the pollution exclusion were meant to address). Other jurisdictions give the term a very broad meaning. One state limits the meaning of release to intentional releases only.

4. **The pollution exclusion is limited to five specific operations, locations, activities, or insureds.** One of the main reasons the absolute pollution exclusion is not absolute is because it is

limited to only five situations or conditions.

5. **There are exceptions to two of the five specific exclusions.** Eight exceptions apply to the five specific exclusions. Six are explicit in the form; one is implied from the policy wording; and one is understood and created due to the lack of any exclusionary wording in the exclusion itself.

Each of these five self-limiting factors is discussed in the upcoming paragraphs, but not necessarily in the order presented. Self-limiting factors 4. and 5. are combined and discussed first, followed by an overview of the "arising out of ..." requirement. The chapter ends with a combined analysis of self-limiting factors 2. and 3. as they both relate to court interpretations.

Five Specific Exclusions

Review of the absolute pollution exclusion reveals that it is very specific regarding what is excluded. The exclusion is insured specific, location specific, activity specific and operations specific. The five exclusions under 2.f.(1) are paraphrased here.

1. A pollution release at or from any premises, site or location which is or ever was owned or occupied by, rented to or loaned to any insured. This is an insured and location specific exclusion known as the owner/occupier exclusion. Current and past pollution incidents, including long-tail claims for prior owners or

occupiers of a property (potentially responsible parties), are effectively deleted by this exclusion. There are three exceptions to this exclusion, but only two apply to the building owner/occupier.

2. A release of pollutants at or from any premises, site or location which is or has ever been used to manage waste. Manage means to handle, store, dispose of, or process. This is a location-specific and operation-specific exclusion with no explicit exceptions making it nearly absolute. Water treatment plants, dumps, and possibly recycling centers are subject to this part of the exclusion depending on the jurisdiction's definition of a pollutant and release.

3. Pollution release during the transportation or management of waste by the insured or anyone else on behalf of the insured. Management here means handled, stored, treated, disposing, or processing. An activity-specific exclusion, this precludes coverage for insureds such as asbestos removal contractors. The exclusion has no exceptions, making it, in a sense, absolute.

4. The release of a pollutant at or from any premises, site or location on which the insured (a contractor and not the owner of the site), or any of the insured's contractors or subcontractors are working (performing operations). Because of exclusion 3. above, this relates to contractors not specifically involved in managing pollution or waste (for example, a regular artisan or

trade-type contractor) making this the contractor's exclusion. Notice this is an operation-specific and location-specific exclusion. Four express exceptions and one implied exception apply to this exclusion, giving coverage back under specific circumstances.

5. Pollution release at or from any premises, site or location the insured contractor or any of its contractors or subcontractors is performing operations if those operations are related to the management of pollutants. Thus, this is an activity-specific exclusion that has no exceptions making it nearly absolute.

Note that this list of exclusions mentions only seven exceptions. This discussion already indicated that there are eight exceptions. There is one exception that applies to the entire exclusion and is not limited to any one particular exclusion; it is understood due to its conspicuous absence from the list of exclusions. This exception is discussed in more detail in an upcoming section.

Coverage denials and court cases related to pollution and the applicability of the absolute pollution exclusion most often revolve around the above five exclusions; but there are two more exclusions related to clean up and government suits for pollution incidents. Paragraph 2.f.(2) addresses these exclusions and the exception to these exclusions.

(2) Any loss, cost or expense arising out of any:

a) Request, demand, order or statutory or regulatory requirement that any insured or others test for,

> *monitor, clean up remove, contain, treat, detoxify or neutralize, or in any way respond to, or assess the effects of, "pollutants"; or*
>
> b) *Claim or "suit" by or on behalf of a governmental authority for damages because of testing for, monitoring, cleaning up, removing, containing, treating, detoxifying, or neutralizing or in any way responding to, or assessing the effects of "pollutants".*
>
> *However, this paragraph does not apply to liability for damages because of "property damage" that the insured would have in the absence of such request, demand, order or statutory or regulatory requirement, or such claim or "suit" by or on behalf of a governmental authority.*

Essentially this section excludes all costs associated with testing, monitoring, cleaning up, etc. whether completed by or paid for by the insured directly; or completed or paid for by the government and billed back to the insured. This is a business risk exclusion with an exception for a nonbusiness risk loss.

The exception gives back property damage coverage (no bodily injury) when the insured causes damage that is covered by one of the exceptions to the pollution exclusion. Cleanup costs are generally considered part of the damages and would have to be paid even if there was no demand or order from a governmental authority.

Cleanup Cost Exclusion Claim Example

The following is an example claim where the cleanup cost Exclusion (2.f.(2)) applies. As it happens, this loss also invokes exclusion 2.f.(1)(a), the owner/occupant exclusion. The subject loss involves a fire at a building housing a cleaning supplies company.

An early morning fire erupted and nearly destroyed a building owned and occupied by a cleaning supplies operation. Specifically, the supplies were for public schools and included cleaning products commonly considered pollutants when not used as designed or when they escaped from their containers.

Due to the heat of the fire and the actions of the fire department, hundreds, maybe even thousands, of gallons of pollutants escaped their containers and the confines of the building. The chemicals mixed with the runoff water from the fire department and ran into storm drains and onto neighboring properties.

The EPA was on hand almost immediately to assess the situation. Not only did this business owner face the destruction of his business, but he also had to deal with the government agency because of a potential pollution problem.

Under the standard pollution exclusion, there would be no coverage for any pollution-related losses or costs. The owner/occupant exclusion specifically excludes the release of any pollutant at or from any premises owned by the insured; and the cleanup exclusion excludes the cost to clean up the pollutants that escaped (or manage them in some other way).

Since there are no exceptions to these exclusions (as will be seen in the next section), all losses or costs associated with the pollution must be paid by the insured. Alternatively, these costs could be financed by the purchase of a stand-alone pollution policy.

Express Exceptions

As stated previously, there are six stated or express exceptions in the absolute pollution exclusion. Two apply to the owner/occupant exclusion (2.f.(1)(a)) and four relate to the contractor's exclusion (2.f.(1)(d)).

Owner/Occupant Exclusion Express Exceptions

The two express exceptions applying to this exclusion are:

> *2.f.(1)(a)(i): "Bodily injury" if sustained within a building and caused by smoke, fumes, vapor or soot produced by or originating from equipment that is used to heat, cool or dehumidify the building, or equipment that is used to heat water for personal use, by the building's occupants or their guests; or*

> *2.f.(1)(a)(iii): "Bodily injury" or "property damage" arising out of heat, smoke or fumes from a "hostile fire."*

Both exceptions are somewhat self-explanatory. But each is limited in scope. The first applies only to bodily injury (no property damage extension) and is positionally limited to injury sustained within the building. The second exception applies to both bodily injury and property damage but is limited by the definition of a hostile fire. A hostile fire is one that is uncontrollable or is outside of its intended area.

Contractor's Exclusion Express Exceptions

Four express exceptions apply specifically to contractors. One is pulled from the owner/occupant exclusion but specifically relates to contractors providing additional insured status to the building owner or occupant. The first of the three express contractor's exclusions exceptions listed under this specific exclusion is:

> *2.f.(1)(d)(i): "Bodily injury" or "property damage" arising out of the escape of fuels, lubricants or other operating fluids which are needed to perform the normal, electrical, hydraulic or mechanical functions necessary for the operation of "mobile equipment" or its parts, if such fuels, lubricants or other operating fluids escape from a vehicle part designed to hold, store or receive them. This exception does not apply if the "bodily injury" or "property damage" arises out of the intentional discharge, dispersal or release of the fuels, lubricants or other operating fluids, or if such fuels, lubricants or other operating fluids are brought on or to the premises, site or location with the intent that they be discharged, dispersed or released as part of the operations being performed by such insured, contractor or subcontractor; ...*

For this exception to apply, the release must: be unintentional, be released from mobile equipment only, occur at an off premises site, and be at a site at which the insured is actively performing operations (not just storing the equipment).

The second of the three express contractor's exceptions reads:

> **2.f.(1)(d)(ii):** *"Bodily Injury" or "property damage" sustained within a building and caused by the release of gases, fumes or vapors from materials brought into that building in connection with operations being performed by you or on your behalf by a contractor or subcontractor; or...*

Notice that there are several qualifiers in this exception. For the exception to apply and coverage to exist: there must be bodily injury or property damage; the BI and PD must be sustained within a building (not outside of the building); and the materials releasing the gases, fumes or vapors must have some connection to the operations being performed by the contractor.

The third of the three exceptions within the contractor's exclusion is:

> **2.f.(1)(d)(iii):** *"Bodily injury" or "property damage" arising out of heat, smoke or fumes from a "hostile fire".*

A fourth contractor's exclusion express exception may apply, but its applicability is depending upon the building owner's or occupants' additional insured status on the contractor's policy. The exception reads:

> **2.f.(1)(a)(ii):** *"Bodily injury" or "property damage" for which* **you** *may be held liable, if you are a* **contractor** *and the owner or lessee of such premises, site or location has been added to your policy as an* **additional insured** *with respect to your* **ongoing operations** *performed for that additional insured at that premises, site or location and such premises, site or location* **is not and never was** *owned or occupied by, or rented or load to, any insured, other than that additional insured.*[Emphasis added.]

Key terms in this exception indicate its purpose, to protect the insured when they contractually accept liability in a construction contract. A building owner or occupant can be held vicariously liable for the actions of a contractor working on these premises; thus many, if not most, owners/occupiers transfer that liability down to the party closest to the activity and presumably best able to avoid the loss or damage, the contractor.

Notice two primary points of this exception: for it to apply the owner/occupier must first be added to the contractor's policy as an additional named insured and it only applies to ongoing operations.

The last requirement is that the insured contractor does not now and has never owned or occupied the premises (other than to work there). This provision can create problems if the contractor builds a speculative home, occupies it as a model/office, and then sells it. Another coverage gap might be created if the contractor owned the building, sold it, then was hired to do the grading.

Contractor's Exclusions Implied Exception

One implied exception to the contractor's exclusion is found in the express wording in the CGL form. Exclusion 2.f.1.(d) specifically excludes pollution injury or damage:

> *"at or from any premises, site or location on which any insured or any contractors or subcontractors working directly or indirectly on any insured's behalf are performing operations if the 'pollutants' are **brought** on or to the premises, site or location in connection with such operations by such insured, contractor or subcontractor"* (emphasis added).

This means that if the pollutant was not brought to the site by the insured or its subcontractor, injury or damage arising out of pollution and caused by the insured's (or its subcontractor's) operations is covered by the policy.

Coverage is created by the express exception in the exclusion; and this exception makes sense. Why should the insured contractor be punished for something that is already on the site?

Contractor's Exclusion Implied Exception Claim Example

A utility contractor specializing in heavy civil construction was removing old pipes and installing new water and sewage piping for a water treatment facility. One of the pipes being removed ran through a control room. During removal, a large amount of sewage-tainted water gushed from the pipe, damaging some of the computers in the control room.

The CGL carrier denied the claim citing the pollution exclusion because of the sewage in the water. This denial should be contested because the sewage was not brought to the job site by the contractor. (There is a second reason the denial should be contested: the pollutant was not a cause-in-fact of the damage – water that just happened to contain sewage was the cause. This factor is discussed later in the chapter.)

The Lack of Exclusion Exception

Coverage A in the CGL provides protection for the financial consequences of bodily injury and property damage for which the insured is held liable, provided there is no applicable exclusion. The last implied exception in the pollution exclusion is understood and created by the conspicuous absence of any exclusionary wording to the contrary. Products-completed operations injury or damage is not excluded by the pollution exclusion; and since there is no exclusion, coverage exists for pollution losses falling under the products- completed operations coverage definition.

Products Example

Fictitious manufacturer Hazardous Pumps, Inc. (Hazardous) provides a prime example of this exception. Hazardous designs and manufacturers pumps for the sole purpose of moving and controlling the movement of hazardous and dangerous chemicals such as chlorine and liquid fertilizers. If a pump (a product) malfunctions and releases toxic fumes causing injury, there is no exclusion, so coverage would apply under the unendorsed CGL.

Completed Operations Example

Local HVAC contractor Comfort Systems, Inc. (Comfort) can provide a great example of the completed operations part of this exception. Comfort replaced an ancient oil heating system with a modern and efficient HVAC system. As part of this process, and after being told the oil tank was empty, they crimped and welded closed the remaining oil pipe lines from the oil tank.

Two months after the work was completed, one of the welds failed and part of the basement filled with 6 inches of oil because the tank was not empty as had been indicated. The homeowner filed a claim against Comfort. Since this is a completed operations loss (as per the definition in the policy), the claim should be covered under ISO's standard pollution exclusion because the contractor's exclusion specifically states that it applies when the insured is performing operations, not once the work is complete.

What These Exceptions Say

These eight exceptions point to the historical purpose of pollution exclusions. Originally drafted in the mid-1970's in response to the federal environment laws (i.e., the Clean Water Act (CWA), the Resource Conservation and Recovery Act (RCRA), and the Comprehensive Environmental Response, Compensation, and Liability act (CERCLA, also known as Superfund)). The original intent of most standardized pollution exclusions was to exclude the losses arising out of injury or damage from environmental pollution falling under the jurisdiction of these laws (now known as "traditional environmental pollution"). In fact, a 2010 New Jersey Supreme Court ruling, *Nav-Its v. Selective Insurance*, noted that the exclusion's terminology is taken from environmental laws and is intended to be interpreted in light of those laws. But not every state court agrees with the use and interpretation. Current application of this exclusion by many jurisdictions seem to stray from this original intent and purpose.

"Arising out of...": The Self-Limiting Causal Connection Requirement

Pollution is not excluded! Excluded is bodily injury or property damage arising out of or caused by the release of a pollutant. Literally, this means that the mere presence of a pollutant (a term defined in the policy and interpreted by the courts) is not sufficient to trigger the pollution exclusion. The pollutant must be the cause-in-fact of the injury or damage.

For pollution to qualify as the factual cause means that the injury or damage would not have occurred apart from the actions of a pollutant. The pollutant must be the cause of the injury or damage, not just a byproduct of the negligent event or simply present at the time or place of the loss. Any other interpretation of this exclusionary wording makes the absolute pollution exclusion unconscionably broad and coverage nearly illusory.

Apply this key question when analyzing this factor. "Is the injury or damage so far removed from the presence of the pollutant so as to make the application of the absolute pollution exclusion unreasonable?" A slip and fall in a grocery store simply because a hazardous cleaning liquid was spilled on the floor is the classic example that was put forth by several departments of insurance when this exclusion was first introduced. Yes, the chemical is a pollutant, but the injury is caused because the floor is slippery, not because the substance that made it slippery is a pollutant. To apply the absolute pollution exclusion in such a case would be absurd and unreasonable.

Is the Substance a Pollutant? Was There a Release? Effects of the Pollutant and Release Requirements

Courts are often charged with reviewing and comparing the facts of a pollution-related loss with policy language to determine the availability of coverage. The problem is there are distinct differences among the jurisdictions. Some courts narrowly define the pollution exclusion in favor of the insured, while others tend to take a broader view of the policy terms to the benefit of the insurance carrier.

For example, some states specifically define pollutant to universally include solvents and cleaners. Conversely, other states have ruled that solvents and cleaners are not pollutants based on the facts of particular cases.

Such a wide spectrum of jurisdictional rulings makes generalizing the application of the pollution exclusion, at best, extremely difficult and impossible at worst. Local rulings must be studied to properly apply the policy language.

Regardless of the jurisdiction and its application of the pollution exclusion, all courts try to answer two questions.

- Is the substance a pollutant?
- Was there a release, discharge, etc. as that jurisdiction defines it?

Pollutant

A particular substance may not always be defined as a pollutant by the courts. Whether a substance is, in fact, a pollutant hinges on the jurisdiction and the facts of the case. Six fact-based tests are applied to analyze a particular substance's classification as a pollutant in a particular situation.

- What is the nature of the injury causing substance?
- What is the typical usage of the substance? Does the insured   typically use the substance as part of its business or operation or is it necessary for the operation?

- What was the quantity of the discharge?
- Was the substance being used as it was intended to be used?
- Is the substance one that is generally viewed as a pollutant?
- Are there any other factors relevant to the case at hand?

From these six questions the court decides whether or not a particular substance is a pollutant. Coverage remains intact (subject to any other exclusions or conditions) if the substance is not classed as a pollutant. But being classed as a pollutant does not automatically negate coverage. There must still be a causal connection (factor 1) between the presence of the pollutant and the injury or damage for the exclusion to apply.

Release, Escape, Etc.

Defining escape, release, etc. is, once again, jurisdictionally-based. Some narrowly define release or escape as a term of art taken from environmental pollution laws and limit its meaning to escape or release from a location as per the laws. Others broadly define these terms to mean escape or release from a particular system.

If there is no escape, release, etc., the pollution exclusion does not apply. Understanding local case law regarding these definitions is required. But again, the pollution must be the cause-in-fact of the injury or damage to be excluded.

In short, court decisions from external jurisdictions do little to guide agents through the pollution exclusion.

Seemingly the only cases that help are those from the jurisdiction in question.

The Total Pollution Exclusion (CG 21 49)

Although outside the intended scope of this chapter, the Total Pollution Exclusion endorsement requires a brief mention. Some underwriters don't want any perceived exposure to a pollution claim, thus they attach a **Total Pollution Exclusion endorsement** (CG 21 49 or a proprietary form) to the CGL policy.

The intent of this exclusionary endorsement is obviously to remove any coverage for injury or damage caused by the pollutant. Essentially, every pollution event is excluded by this form as there are no exceptions to the exclusion.

Even this broad exclusion holds true to the idea that the proximate cause of the injury or damage must be the pollution for the exclusion to apply. The form reads, in part, "...which would not have occurred in whole or part *but for*..." (emphasis added). "But for" is the proximate cause requirement. In the utility contractor example above, water released due to the negligent actions of the insured was the proximate cause of the damage, not the presence of a pollutant. The damage would have occurred even if pure, clean water was released.

(See Appendix A for a case study on this exclusionary endorsement and its alternatives.)

Conclusion

Remember the absolute pollution exclusion is not absolute as there are five self-limiting factors and eight exceptions.

Anytime a carrier assessing a loss asserts the pollution exclusion, always look for the true cause-in-fact of the loss. The mere presence of a pollutant is not (or should not be) sufficient to trigger the use of the exclusion.

Key Questions

- Is the substance a pollutant?
- Was there a release?
- Does the release fall under one of the five specific exclusions?
- Do any of the exceptions apply to the exclusion?

Chapter 4

Understanding Personal and Advertising Injury Protection – CGL's Coverage Part B

All actions detailed in the definition of Personal and Advertising Injury, as contained in ISO's CGL policy's Coverage B, are intentional acts or offenses. But even though the actions leading to charges of libel, slander, invasion of privacy, copyright infringement, false arrest, defamation, and other listed offenses defined in this section are intentional, the results must be unintentional for Coverage B to respond, defend, and/or pay the defined third-party injury.

Personal and Advertising Injury Coverage – Coverage B is wholly separate from the Bodily Injury and Property Damage protection provided by Coverage A, but Coverage B is fully contained within the package of CGL-provided coverage. This translates to mean that all other CGL policy sections apply equally to Coverage A and Coverage B.

However, Personal and Advertising Injury Coverage is largely ignored by agents. These coverages are rarely highlighted, nor are any risk management steps taken to help the insured avoid these types of losses. Yet, every insured has a Personal and Advertising Injury exposure even though it's not as easy to spot or explain as the bodily injury and property damage exposure covered by Coverage A. Agents set themselves apart by highlighting these real exposures and the available coverage.

Coverage Trigger

Coverage B, although equal in weight (if not importance) to Coverage A, is triggered by an offense rather than an occurrence, as in Coverage A. Personal and Advertising Injury responds only when a listed offense takes place during the policy period.

Offense is not a specifically defined term in the policy. Its meaning is inferred from the definition of personal and advertising injury. Further, Coverage B listed offenses are generally definite in time, with the possible exception of published materials. Because of the timelessness of published materials, many courts and the policy wording appears to place the date of the offense as the date of first publication.

Under Coverage B, the policy in effect when the offense takes place responds to the claim.

Claims-Made Form Differences

The above coverage trigger discussion assumes coverage written on an occurrence basis. When written on an occurrence form, the insured is subject only to any applicable statute of limitations (or repose) in regard to Personal and Advertising Injury Coverage. If the offense took place during the policy period, that policy responds regardless of when the claim is brought. However, if the insure is written on a claims-made form, the offense must additionally be committed after the listed retroactive date (if any).

Breadth of Coverage

Liability protection extended from Coverage B is created, or maybe limited, by definition. Coverage B extends coverage based mainly on the definitions of personal and advertising injury and advertisement.

Personal and Advertising Injury Coverage is functionally equivalent to a named perils property policy. That is, unless the offense causing the loss is specifically named or listed in the definition, there is no coverage. An earlier paragraph noted that an offense (the act that triggers coverage) is not a defined term and must take its lead from the definition that shares its name with this coverage part. These are the offences that make up the definition of Personal and advertising injury. Coverage is limited to these offences.

a) *False arrest, detention, or imprisonment;*

b) *Malicious prosecution;*

c) *The wrongful eviction from, wrongful entry into, or invasion of the right of private occupancy of a room, dwelling or premises that a person occupies, committed by or on behalf of its owner, landlord or lessor;*

d) *Oral or written publication, in any manner, of material that slanders or libels a person or organization or disparages a person's or organization's goods, products or services;*

e) *Oral or written publication, in any manner, of material that violates a person's right of privacy;*

f) The use of another's advertising idea in your "advertisement"; or

g) Infringing upon another's copyright, trade dress or slogan in your "advertisement."

If the insured commits an offense not found in the definition, there is no coverage. And just like named perils property coverage, it is up to the insured to prove the offense is covered by the definition. If the offense is within the definition, then the insured must hope that none of the 16 Coverage B exclusions apply.

Examples of Personal and Advertising Injury Offenses

Personal and Advertising Injury, as indicated above, is equivalent to a named perils coverage. If the injury is not caused by one of the defined causes of loss, listed as offenses, there is no coverage.

The previous section merely listed the perils insured. Below are examples of each of the listed offenses.

Some Offensive Examples

Retail stores, auto repair shops, restaurants or any operation where customers are likely to congregate all have an exposure to false arrest, detention, or imprisonment. Consider a retail shop that suspects a customer of shoplifting. If they detain the suspect and then discover they have the wrong person, the insured may be guilty of false detention (unless there is an individual allowed to effect arrest, then it's actually false arrest). Consider also an auto repair shop that refuses to replace a tire so that the customer can leave. Depending on the circumstances, that could also be false detention. The examples are numerous, but the gist is that anytime the insured holds someone against his will and without cause, the insured may be guilty of this offense. Certain clients have a far greater exposure to this offense, such as security companies and private police contractors. Strict risk management guidelines for accusing and detaining customers or suspects must be developed and closely followed.

Charges of malicious prosecution can be leveled against any insured that brings a civil or criminal suit against another without merit. In order for the injured party to charge malicious prosecution, there must be malice on the part of the insured and the verdict must be in favor of the injured person. Any insured charged with suing another person or entity to harass (or for revenge) is covered by the Personal and Advertising Injury protection, subject to exclusions.

Insureds providing long-term or short-term living quarters are subject to charges of wrongful eviction from, wrongful entry into or invasion of right of private occupancy. This is not limited to lessors and landlords. Such charges can also be leveled against hotels and motels. The invasion of a person's right to inhabit any living area is a covered offense.

Libel, slander and defamation can be charged against nearly any insured. For example, in an effort to sway a new account, suppose an agent makes a false statement about his competitor; or during a jobsite argument, the plumbing contractor yells at the top of his longs that the HVAC contractor is a "lying, cheating scoundrel" while several people are within earshot. Any written or oral statement that disparages another person, organization or product (true or not) could lead to charges of libel, slander, or defamation.

Privacy rights have taken center stage in recent years. Insureds may have in their possession incredible amounts of private information: Social Security numbers, medical information, driving history, etc. If any of this information is published, thus making it available to an unintended party, the insured could be sued. It's the publication of this information that triggers Coverage B. However, publication is not defined in the policy, but its everyday meaning connotes that act of making something public.

One question often arises when such personal information is stored on a computer system. If the system is hacked, is such loss (theft) of private information covered under the Personal and Advertising Injury Coverage part? It is not likely that Coverage B would respond to this loss. Merely having the information stolen is not contemplated in the idea or definition of publication. To have coverage for losing or having the information stolen requires a different type of coverage.

Beyond personal data, violating a person's right of privacy may include the use of their pictures or likenesses in an advertisement, posting their picture without consent, or maybe even the posting of insufficient-fund checks (subject to state laws). Everyone has the right to manage the use of their own information and image. Any violation of that right can lead to charges of violating privacy rights.

Insurance agents, lawyers, and doctors are prime examples of insured with this exposure. Each has large amounts of personal client-specific information in their possession.

The last two Personal and Advertising Injury offenses relate to advertising: using another person's or entity's advertising idea, or infringing on another copyright, trade dress or slogan in an advertisement. A hotel advertises, "We'll leave the lights on for you" or a cell phone network ad claims, "So quiet you can hear a pin drop." Lifting another corporation's slogans is one example of the coverage provided to this part of the definition. Using a logo, theme, or any other element of advertising in an attempt to confuse those seeing the advertisement are other examples of this covered offense.

Application of the Current Coverage B Exclusions

If the committed offense falls within the Personal and Advertising Injury definition discussed above, the offense must be compared against the 16 exclusions that apply to the coverage. Each of the current exclusions is discussed individually in the following paragraphs, with a particular emphasis on the embedded exceptions.

Knowing Violation of Rights of Another (exclusion 2.a.)

Individuals and entities have certain rights: privacy, truth (not being unjustly defamed), occupancy, personal safety, freedom of movement, use of ideas or innovation, property rights and others. Not all rights, however defined, are covered within the definition of personal and advertising injury.

Two important conditions must be met for this exclusion to apply: the insured must knowingly violate another's rights and such violation must be by or at the direction of the insured. If the insured is unaware that the action violated or might violate the person's or entity's rights, the offense is not excluded. Likewise, an employee acting outside the acceptable and expected scope of employment does not preclude coverage for any other insured. Vicarious liability protection is extended to the insured entity as the exclusion only applies if the action was done by or at the direction of the insured. The first incarnation of this exclusion was in the 1998 edition of the form.

Material Published with Knowledge of Falsity (exclusion 2.b)

Published, as used in this exclusion, constitutes any oral or written communication. Like exclusion 2.a. above, the exclusion applies if two conditions are met. The insured knows that the information is false. The publication is by (or at the direction) of the insured. Coverage for misplaced trust in information provided by a usually good source and vicarious employer liability is preserved by the wording.

Material Published Prior to Policy Period (exclusion 2.c.)

No coverage exists for any oral or written publication first broadcast or published before the current policy period. This particular exclusion limits coverage to the policy in effect when the offense takes place. This avoids the possibility that several policies will be called upon to pay for one specific offense or claim. This also avoids the stacking of limits.

Criminal Acts (exclusion 2.d.)

Unlike exclusion 2.a., which excludes intentional violation of civil (individual) rights, this excludes criminal (acts against the public) wrongs. The extent of this exclusion has changed and expanded, some consider drastically, to include vicarious liability protection for the insured entity. Prior wording excluded criminal acts if committed by any insured. Current policy language (which first appeared in the 2001 edition) excludes criminal acts only if committed by or at the direction of the insured. Criminal acts can range from misdemeanor offenses to felony actions leading to a defined personal and advertising injury. For example, a landlord that incorrectly evicts an individual may be charged with breaking and entering, a criminal act, in addition to wrongful eviction (a civil act with the personal and advertising injury definition). The insurance carrier will not defend the criminal charges even though they may defend the civil charges (two separate courts).

Contractual Liability (exclusion 2.e.)

Coverage A (Bodily Injury and Property Damage) and Coverage B (Personal and Advertising Injury) both exclude liability assumed in and arising solely from a contract (if liability would exist in the absence of the contract, the policy will pay regardless of the presence of a contract). But unlike Coverage A, Personal and Advertising Injury Coverage contains no contractual exceptions. Coverage A excepts insured contracts from the exclusion while Coverage B does not contain such an exception. Any insured assuming another's personal or advertising injury liability by contract does so at their own risk as there is no protection extended from the policy.

Contracts can present a unique challenge in regards to this exclusion, especially construction contracts. The legal profession lumps several injury types into one term, personal injury. In contrast, the insurance industry correctly uses two terms to describe different injuries, bodily injury and personal injury. Because of this difference, agents may find contracts requesting the insured to indemnify and hold a party harmless for personal injury. Likely, the attorney intends the meaning to be bodily injury, but since the terms do not agree with policy language, a gap could arise (for both Coverage A and Coverage B).

Contractual risk transfer and negotiating/correcting contract provisions is outside the intended scope of this chapter, but agents need to be aware of this contractual exclusion. There are only two possible solutions. Convince the underwriter to remove the exclusion (not likely to happen). Attach the **Limited Contractual Liability Coverage for Personal and Advertising Injury** endorsement (CG 22 74). Unfortunately, the CG 22 74 extends contractual liability protection under personal and advertising injury to only the offenses of false arrest, detention or imprisonment (the first defined offense).

Breach of Contract (exclusion 2.f.)

A breach of contract arises when one party to the contract is deprived of certain promised benefits or protection due to the other party's unintentional or intentional failure to comply with the contractual agreement. The exclusion's exception may offer a clue regarding its application in relation to personal and advertising injury coverage. Violation of *"an implied contract to use another's advertising in your advertisement"* is excepted from the breach of contract exclusion. Comparing the breach of contract exception with the named peril coverage offered in the personal and advertising injury definition, it appears that the exclusion's main focus is the misappropriation of another's advertising in violation of a specific contract.

Consider this example. An insurance carrier gives an agency contractual permission to distribute advertising or promotional materials containing the company logo, but only in the agent's state of domicile. The campaign proves so successful that the agent distributes the material in two surrounding states. Distribution outside the contractually permitted area is a breach of contract and is not covered by the policy. If, however, the agent calls the carrier's marketing department and asks if he can distribute material with its logo, and the carrier says it's acceptable (with no explicit instructions), any suit that arises because the agent distributed outside the state of domicile is covered as there was an implied contract of use in any manner desired.

Quality or Performance of Goods – Failure to Conform to statements (exclusion 2.g.)

This does not equate to a products liability exclusion. Personal and Advertising Injury coverage has nothing to do with the product itself. It's the effect on an individual's or entity's reputation caused by false or faulty advertising that is excluded. A local hardware store, for example, in an attempt to sell its inventory of Acme edgers and trimmers, runs an ad that reads, "Acme edgers and trimmers are guaranteed to make your yard green and weed-free." An edger or trimmer is unlikely (perhaps impossible) to make the user's yard green and weed-free. Therefore, the product will not live up to its advertising. Any customer demands for money or suits against the manufacturer or hardware store will be denied under Coverage B, as will Acme's suit against the hardware store for damaging its reputation by improper use of its product and trademark in an advertisement.

Wrong Description of Prices (exclusion 2.h.)

There are two reasons for this exclusion: bait and switch, the practice of deliberately advertising artificially low prices or artificially high inventories to entice shoppers to visit the store, then attempting to sell them high priced articles using spurious tactics, is considered false advertising and is illegal and advertising goods is a business decision, and incorrectly printed pricing is a business risk not covered by insurance.

Infringement of Copyright, Patent, Trademark or Trade Secret (exclusion 2.i.)

Created and added to clarify the insurance industry's intent to not provide coverage for violating the intellectual property (IP) rights of another. Using and taking credit for someone else's IP amounts to an intentional act and is also a business risk. Plus, specialized policies are available to defend the insured against these charges.

However, an insured's use of and infringement upon another's IP in its advertising is not excluded in the current policy wording. Copying the look and feel of another entity's ad is not excluded. For example, running an ad featuring two actors dressed like cavemen talking about your insurance agency, even though the agency is not related to GEICO, would be an infringement of a trade dress character, but would still be covered under the CGL. However, calling the agency GEICO would be excluded.

There is an important change in terminology between the exclusion title and the exception to the exclusion. The form excludes violation of a trademark but gives back coverage for use of another's trade dress in the insured's advertising. A trademark is a name or slogan specific and identifiable as pertaining to a particular product. Use of a trademarked product or name in an advertisement is not protected by the policy (this is why ads use the term facial tissue rather than Kleenex®). Conversely, use of a trade dress in an advertisement is protected. Trade dress has to do with the overall, distinctive image of the product; and it must be

something that is nonfunctional. This is why use of the
cavemen by another agency is protected: they are associated
with the GEICO brand and definitely distinctive, but they are
not a functional part of the name or operation of GEICO the
company.

An interesting fact about a trademark: a trademark and its
protection arises out of use, not necessarily or exclusively
registration. Food Lion, a large grocery store chain, was known
as Food Town until it tried to enter Johnston County, N.C.
Clayton, a town in the northeast part of the county, already
had a long-existing local grocery store known as Food Town. It
sued the larger chain and forced the name change because it
had rights to the use of the name, even though it was not large
and the name was not registered with anyone other than the
North Carolina secretary of state.

Insureds in Media and Internet Type Businesses (exclusion 2.j.)

The exclusion's title says it all. There is no personal or
advertising injury protection for any entity in the publishing,
web, or Internet business. One reason is the named peril type
of coverage extended by this coverage part is inadequate to
cover these businesses' exposures. Another reasons is that the
exposure for entities engaged in these types of businesses has
moved from one of general liability to the level of professional
liability. A media professional liability policy is the appropriate
method to protect entities engaged in media and Internet
operations.

Four exceptions to the 2.j. exclusion require mention. The first three, found in **Section V – Definitions**, provide coverage for: false arrest, detention, or imprisonment (14.a.); malicious prosecution (14.b.); and wrongful eviction, entry or invasion of private occupancy (14.c.). The final exception found in the exclusion itself states that *"the placing of frames, borders or links, or advertising, for you or others anywhere on the Internet, is not by itself, considered the business of advertising, broadcasting, publishing or telecasting."* Such work has to be the major source of income to be considered "in the business of...."

Electronic Chatrooms or Bulletin Boards (exclusion 2.k.)

A chat room is a real-time group of people using instant messaging to communicate; the rooms are usually divided or arranged by topic. A bulletin board is better thought of as a forum or message board. Users generally post questions, answer existing questions, or respond to answers on their own schedule without having to be there the same time other people are posting. Any personal or advertising injury resulting from or arising out of these facilities is excluded if the insured hosts, owns or controls the rooms or forums. Merely posting to (or being a part of) a conversation is not grounds for exclusion; the insured must, in some way, control the facility.

Unauthorized Use of Another's Name or Product (exclusion 2.l.)

Specifically, this exclusion eliminates coverage should the insured use another entity's name or product name in its e-mail address, domain name, or metatag, or any other tactics meant to mislead buyers. A copy machine retailer, for example, can't use "Xerox" in its web address, e-mail address, or in any other such manner (unless specifically licensed and contractually permitted to by the subject company). The purpose of such use is generally to bring the customer to the insured's site (real or virtual) by false pretense.

Pollution (exclusion 2.m.): and Pollution-Related (exclusion 2.n.)

ISO divided these into two separate exclusions in the 2001 CGL edition. Prior to this division, both were part of the same exclusion. Essentially, any personal or advertising injury related to any type of release, clean up, or testing related to pollution is excluded.

War (exclusion 2.o.)

Specifically excludes any personal and advertising injury arising out of war whether declared, undeclared or simply war-like. While this seems like an odd personal and advertising injury exclusion, it is important to note when it was introduced: after 9/11/2001. After 9/11, false arrest, detention, or imprisonment of individuals meeting certain visual profiles became very possible. Entities that perform background checks, surveillance, or investigation may also be subject to charges of violation of a person's right of privacy (discussed earlier). How that will play out in the war on terrorism is yet unknown, especially if the individual is a person of interest.

Distribution of Materials in Violation of Statutes (exclusion 2.p.)

This last exclusion was created in response to the CAN-SPAM Act of 2003 and somewhat to the Telephone Consumer Protection Act (TCPA) which limited access to consumers by solicitors trying to sell them goods, products, or services. These laws gave rise to the no-call requirements on telemarketers and really to any cold-call-to-consumer-operations in business today.

CAN-SPAM was signed into law on December 16, 2003. It's an acronym that stands for: **C**ontrolling the **A**ssault of **N**on-**S**olicited **P**ornography **A**nd **M**arketing Act of 2003. The TCPA was first signed into law in 1991 (amending the Communications Act of 1934) and was modified by the CAN-SPAM Act. Portions of the TCPA dealt with unsolicited fax advertising. On July 9, 2005, the Junk Fax Prevention Act of 2005 was signed. This act can impose hefty fines on violators of the law (up to $500 per page). Violation of these laws can be rather expensive, and the costs are not covered by insurance.

Prior to the addition of exclusion 2.p. in the CGL, insurers attached the CG 00 67, **Exclusion—Violation of Statutes That Govern E-Mails, Fax, Phone Calls or Other Methods of Sending Material or Information.**

Conclusion

Agents desiring to stand out need to understand this coverage part, point out the exposures, and manage the risk. Insureds may have exposures that require additional or alternate protection. Even if they choose to not purchase the additional protection, the agent has done his duty, pointed out the exposure/option, and protected his errors and omissions exposure.

Key Questions

- Is the offense included within the definition of personal and advertising injury?
- Do any of the 16 exclusions apply to the offense?
- Are there any exceptions to the exclusions giving back coverage?

Chapter 5
The Difference Between the OCP and the CGL

"Why would any agent make such a ridiculous recommendation?" That was my response when I read that an agent had recommended to a general contractor that he drop his commercial general liability (CGL) policy and instead write owners and contractors protective liability (OCP) coverage for each project and location. No reasonable and prudent agent would make this recommendation; but maybe that's the answer right there.

An OCP is not equivalent to the CGL; its closest comparison is the coverage granted to only the additional insured when the CG 20 10 (**Additional Insured—Owners, Lessees or Contractors**) is attached to the commercial general liability policy. Even in this case, the CGL with the CG 20 10 is broader in some areas.

Who is Protected by the OCP?

The first OCP concept that must be fully understood is that the party that pays for the policy is not the policy's named insured. Once grasped, the limited use and purpose of the OCP becomes evident.

Owners and contractors protective (OCP) liability forms are purchased by a general contractor or lower tier contractor for the sole purpose of protecting a person or entity holding a higher position in the construction hierarchy. No coverage is extended from the OCP to the lower tier contractor that paid for the protection. The lower tier contractor that purchases the coverage is listed in the policy as the covered contractor, not as the named insured. This relationship between buyer and coverage is equivalent to the upper tier contractor being named as an additional insured on the lower tier contractor's CGL.

Coverage Provided by the OCP

Only two types of coverage are extended from the OCP liability policy: vicarious liability and coverage for negligent supervision of the named contractor. No other protection is provided by this limited form.

Vicarious Liability

Vicarious liability is one party's liability for the actions of another party. Such liability can arise out of a relationship (parent/ child, employer/employee, etc.), position, or contract. The first party's right, ability, or duty to control the actions of another party can lead to it being held vicariously liable. No entity can be held liable for the actions of another if they lack the opportunity or responsibility to control those actions.

Owners or general contractors hold a certain amount of control over the actions of lower tier contractors. This control leaves them vulnerable to being held vicariously liable for the actions of these lower-level entities. Such vulnerability creates the need for contractual risk transfer and some form of insurance protection (accomplished by being the named insured on an OCP or by being added as an additional insured to the CGL). The OCP policy, in general terms, states that the policy pays for bodily injury or property damage caused by an occurrence arising out of "operations performed for you by the 'contractor' at the location specified in the Declarations."

As is the customary use of the term, the "you" of the OCP is the named insured; but the "you" did not pay for the policy, as described above, the contractor did. Knowing each party's role within the OCP's coverage points to the policy's narrow protection.

If the contractor's operations cause injury to a third party or damage to a third party's property, the OCP responds to protect the "you" of the policy, but only if that "you" is somehow held liable for the actions of the contractor. Notice the policy does not protect the "you" for its own actions; nor does it protect the contractor for its own injurious actions.

The OCP responds when, for example, the named insured (the property owner or higher tier contractor) is held liable because the named "contractor" (the purchaser of the policy) negligently knocks over a wall and kills three workers not related to the contractor. This is only one example of the extent of vicarious liability.

Negligent Supervision

Conversely, the second provision does extend coverage for the named insured's own actions, or in this case, improper actions. The OCP provides coverage for, "Your acts or omissions in connection with the general supervision of such operations."

Owners and/or general contractors retain certain non-delegable duties. One, among others, is proper supervision of the work methods employed by subcontractors on the job site. Another is a duty to maintain the site, to keep it free of hazards, or protect the public against hazards that cannot be avoided (for example, putting a barrier around an open hole).

If the owner or general contractor fails to properly supervise the activities of the specifically-listed contractor, and bodily injury or property damage occurs as a result, the OCP responds. Coverage is not extended to protect against any and all charges of negligent supervision. The OCP covers the "you" against liability arising out of negligent supervision of only the contractor named in the policy. While this is a benefit to the owner or general contractor, there is still no benefit for the contractor that purchased the policy.

This coverage provision is no broader than that provided by the owner's or general contractor's CGL. In fact, it is not as broad as the coverage extended from the owner's or GC's own CGL policy since it is limited to a single contractor.

Major Gaps in the OCP

Beyond the limited protection detailed above, the OCP is lacking in many other areas when compared to the coverage provided by the CGL policy. In addition to the fact that the OCP extends no coverage to the purchaser of the policy. There are four coverage and limit gaps.

1. **No Products-Completed Operations Protection**. The OCP provides only premises/operations coverage; once the work at the site is complete, protection ends. Exclusion C and the fact that there is no products/completed operations definition are proof.

2. **No Personal/Advertising Injury Coverage.** Since the OCP is intended to extend coverage only for the insured's liability arising out of the operations of the contractor, there is no coverage for personal and advertising injury. Coverage can be added by endorsement (CG 28 05).

3. **Problems with Excess Coverage**. The insured's umbrella or excess policy will not sit on top of the OCP because the buyer is not the named insured. If limits in addition to those provided are required, the contractor (buyer) would be required to purchase an excess OCP policy.

4. **Narrow Definition of Insured Contract**. The OCP's definition of insured contract does not include the business contract provision (9.f in the CGL).

This missing provision is somewhat reasonable because the OCP is a known-parties, closed policy. This means that the policy only responds if the first party (the named insured) is held liable for the actions of a specific second party (the contractor that purchased the policy). These are the only two parties that matter. The policy is not intended to allow the named insured to pick up, via contract, the tort liability of another party.

Comparing the OCP with Additional Insured Status

An OCP policy does no more than extend additional insured status to the property owner or general contractor requesting the coverage. There is no coverage for the named insured's own actions and no coverage extended to the entity that pays for the protection (defined in the policy as the contractor).

For its length, the OCP doesn't provide as much protection to the upper tier contractor as it would enjoy if it was scheduled as an additional insured on the lower tier contractor's CGL using the CG 20 10. As per the coverage gaps listed above, the OCP is a poor substitute for additional insured status. Only one of the four gaps is common to both the OCP and the CG 20 10: the lack of products/completed operations coverage. However, this gap can be fixed in the CGL by attachment of the CG 20 37; there is no such fix for the OCP.

Some insurance practitioners claim that it is better to provide an OCP liability policy to the entity requesting additional insured status to ensure that there are adequate limits for a loss and that any loss involving the additional insured does not reduce the aggregate limits. The potential problem associated with aggregate limits is solved by attachment of the CG 25 03 **Designated Construction Project(s) General Aggregate Limited**; and the idea that any loss might be increased by the involvement of the additional insured is fallacious. There is only one injury, and it doesn't matter how many parties are being charged, the injured party can only be paid *once* for his injuries.

Proper Use of an OCP

Some property owners or general contractors might desire the minor coverage extension provided by the OCP for their negligent supervision of the named contractor. Being able to access this protection negates the property owner's or general contractor's need to look to their own CGL for this protection. Beyond this, there is little difference between the OCP and additional insured status.

Owners and contractors' protective liability is rarely seen or even requested for good reason. It's a single-purpose form whose coverage can be mimicked by other, more common means. Rarely should an OCP be seen as a primary choice.

An OCP should never be used in place of a commercial general liability policy. Doing so would remove all coverage for the actions of the contractor or subcontractor. OCPs are intended to protect someone other than the entity that bought the coverage. To assure coverage for ongoing and completed operations, the entity must have a CGL policy.

Chapter 6

Contractual Risk Transfer Coverage Extended from the Unendorsed CGL

Vicarious liability is created when one person or entity is (or can be) held legally liable for the results of another person's or entity's actions. Such indirect liability can arise out of a relationship (parent/child, employer/employee, etc.), position, or contract. Also required is the right, ability, or duty to control the actions of the directly liable party. Without the opportunity or responsibility to control another's actions, there can be no vicarious liability.

Owners and general contractors hold a position with a certain amount of control over, and responsibility for, the actions of lower tier contractors. That control leaves them vulnerable to being held vicariously liable for the actions of these lower-level entities in addition to their liability for their own actions.

Avoidance of, or the attempted avoidance of, the financial consequences that can result from being held vicariously liable for the actions or inactions of another is an understandable and acceptable reason for the use of contractual risk transfer. Indemnity and waiver of subrogation agreements, which constitute contractual risk transfer, are, or should be, the upper tier contractor's attempt to avoid or lessen the vicarious liability exposure created by lower tier contractors. Questions of contract enforceability arise when the upper tier contractor attempts to contractually exculpate themselves from liability for their sole actions.

Contractual risk transfer is wholly separate from the contractual requirements to purchase or provide insurance protection. Upper tier contractors become so focused on enforcing contractual insurance requirements that they ignore the breadth of contractually assumed risk already taken on in the lower tier contractor's Commercial General Liability (CGL) policy. Transferors (upper tier contractors) should concern themselves more with the basic CGL than with the endorsements they so fervently pursue.

This chapter describes the protection extended to an indemnitee by the unendorsed CGL. For sake of reference, the 04 13 version of the basic CGL and the CG 20 10 is used in the following discussion.

Automatic Contractually Accepted Risk

Three parts of the unendorsed CGL policy define the protection and coverage limits extended to transferors (indemnitees): the exception to the Contractual Liability exclusion, the definition of insured contract and the Supplementary Payments section of the policy. The exception gives coverage; the definition defines or limits coverage; and the supplementary payments provisions may act to expand the limits of coverage available to indemnitees. Notice that the overall breadth of protection extended by the CGL to contractual indemnitees hangs on the definition of insured contract.

Exception to the Contractual Liability Exclusion (2.b.)

There are two exceptions to the contractual liability exclusion, but only one involves contractually accepted liability. Exception (2) describes the parameters by which contractual liability is covered in the CGL; protection is provided when all four of these conditions are met.

- The liability is assumed by an insured contract.
- The bodily injury or property damage occurs after the execution of the contract.
- Defense and other fees are assumed in the contract (indemnify and hold harmless wording required).
- A suite alleges injury or damage covered by the policy.

At this point defense costs and any other fees relating to the indemnitee are within the limits of coverage, lowering the available limits. But provisions within the supplementary payments section can serve to negate this limitation.

Definition of Insured Contract

Subpart f. of the unaltered CGL's definition of insured contract extends liability coverage to contractual indemnitees when required by contract; but only for the transferor's tort liability. A tort in this context is a negligent act leading to charges of bodily injury or property damage. Again, the indemnitee is only covered for action covered by the policy. In essence, if the named insured would be covered by the policy, so would the indemnitee.

Notice that the definition does not limit the level of risk transfer accepted; it simply states, *"That part of any other contract or agreement pertaining to your business ... under which you assume the tort liability of another party to pay for 'bodily injury' or 'property damage' to a third person or organization."* The level of transfer could only be limited by statute when the unendorsed wording is in use; this is or can be broader than the wording allowed by the CG 20 10.

Insurers routinely alter the definition of insured contract by use of one of two available endorsements:

- Contractual Liability Limitation (CG 21 39)
- Amendment of Insured Contract (CG 24 26)

The CG 21 39 should be avoided when possible. This endorsement removes subpart f. from the definition of insured contract, thus removing all protection normally extended to indemnitees. Allowing this endorsement's attachment can lead to the insured lower tier contractor's breach of contract under the construction contract's indemnification agreement, especially in the absence of other endorsements (i.e., additional insured endorsements).

Essentially, the **Amendment of Insured Contract** endorsement (CG 24 26) redefines the meaning of insured contract to match the coverage granted to the Additional Insured in the CG 20 10. By adding the phrase, *"provided the 'bodily injury' or 'property damage' is caused, in whole or in* *part, by you or by those acting on your behalf,"* the CG 24 26 mimics the additional insured wording. Such phraseology excludes the possibility of the indemnitor's assumption of the indemnitee's sole negligence; the named insured must somehow be directly or vicariously liable for the actions, either individually or in contribution with another party.

Of the two insured contract definition-altering endorsements, the CG 24 26 is obviously preferred. However, if the CGL can be written without either endorsement, the broadest coverage is ex- tended to the indemnitee.

Extending completed operations protection to the upper tier contractor to protect it against vicarious liability for injury or damage caused by the inferior work of the lower tier contractor can be the source of long debates with underwriters and the upper tier contractor's risk management department. Some contracts continue to request the 11 85 version of the CG 20 10 or its equivalent. Well, there is no equivalent, even when the CG 20 37 is attached.

Most of these conversations, debates, and hassles can be avoided if the definition of insured contract remains unaltered. Notice again the wording of subpart f. as presented above. All that is required is that the named insured assume the tort liability of one party to pay an injured third party. If the contract specifically states that the lower tier contractor is to indemnify and hold the upper tier contractor harmless against liability for bodily injury or property damage arising out of the structure once it has been put to its intended use, then the exception to the exclusion and the definition of insured contract combine to extend completed operations coverage to the indemnitee (upper tier contractor).

As stated, such coverage hinges on the definition of insured contract; all the more reason for agents to avoid any redefining endorsement. The insured meets his contractual requirement as long as coverage is in force and the definition is not altered. If the definition is altered at renewal, such could be considered a material change to coverage requiring the carrier to notify the insured and the agent to discuss the change with the insured.

Supplementary Payments

All coverage for contractually assumed liability extended from the unendorsed CGL is provided by the exception to the contractual liability exclusion and the definition of insured contract. However, the supplementary payments section addresses the issue of limits available for the defense and protection of the indemnitee.

If certain conditions are met, defense costs and fees associated with the defense of the indemnitee are in addition to the limit rather than included within the limit of coverage, thus avoiding the reduction in limits discussed above. Defense for the indemnitee (transferor) is in addition to the limits of coverage if the following conditions are met.

- The BI or PD suit names both the insured and the indemnitee as defendants.
- The suit seeks damages assumed by the insured in an insured contract.

- The liability policy applies to the damage.
- The liability for such defense and other costs are assumed in the contract.
- There is no conflict of interest between the insured and he indemnitee.
- The indemnitee agrees to let the insurer control the defense and choice of counsel.
- The indemnitee fully cooperates with the insurer (a long list of duties.)

Lack any of these requirements at any point in the process and the cost of defending the indemnitee returns again to being paid as part of and within the coverage limits.

Key Questions

- Has the definition of insured contract been altered by endorsement?
- When was the construction contract executed?
- When did the injury or damage occur?
- Have you reviewed the contract?
- Does the suit allege damage covered by the policy?
- Have all the supplementary payment conditions been met?

Chapter 7

Three CGL Endorsements
Every Insured Should Avoid

Endorsements to the CGL policy are highly specialized. A high percentage are either exclusionary or extend protection to distinct classes of additional insureds. Most of the remaining endorsements alter coverage for only a limited class or type of insured or are state-specific. Discount the above CGL endorsement classes and only a few remain that extend beneficial additional coverage to an insured, and even fewer can be considered usable across the spectrum of all insureds.

Among the CGL's exclusionary endorsements are three every insured should absolutely avoid whenever possible. Occasionally underwriters are unwilling (or unable) to forego some level of exclusion or limitation, so, where applicable, alternatives to these exclusionary endorsements are provided. The three exclusions every insured should avoid are the: **Total Pollution Exclusion Endorsement** (CG 21 49), **Contractual Liability Limitation** (CG 21 39) and **Limitation of Coverage to Designated Premises or Project** (CG 21 44).

Total Pollution Exclusion Endorsement

The pollution exclusion in the unendorsed CGL is known as the absolute pollution exclusion. This is obviously misnamed since the unaltered wording does provide some coverage via exceptions to the exclusions. Some suggest "broad form pollution exclusion" might be a better name for the removal of coverage accomplished by the unaltered wording. (See Chapter 3 for more detail on the absolute pollution exclusion wording.)

Regardless of the terminology used to describe the unendorsed exclusion, some underwriters do not wish to provide coverage for any pollution event and accomplish this desire by attaching the **Total Pollution Exclusion Endorsement** (CG 21 49). Essentially every pollution event is excluded by this endorsement. However, there is still one pseudo exception to this exclusion: the pollution must be the proximate cause of the loss, not just present at the time of injury (see Appendix A: "Insurer is 'Torturing' Policy Using Pollution Exclusion to Deny Death Claims").

Convincing the underwriter to remove this exclusion may be nearly impossible. If unable to negotiate the exclusion away, offer one of two alternatives: the **Total Pollution Exclusion with a Building Heating, Cooling and Dehumidifying Equipment Exception and a Hostile Fire Exception** (CG 21 65) or the **Total Pollution Exclusion with a Hostile Fire Exception** (CG 21 55). Both endorsements are still exclusions, but they give back coverage for some injury or damage resulting from an otherwise excluded pollution event. CG 21 65 gives back coverage, by exception to the exclusion, for injury or damage caused by pollution originating from an HVAC system or arising out of a hostile fire. The CG 21 55 gives back coverage for injury or damage caused by pollution resulting from a hostile fire. A hostile fire is defined in the CGL as a fire which becomes uncontrollable or breaks out from where it was intended to be.

Obviously the first choice is to have the exclusion removed completely. Failing that, ask first for the CG 21 65 and lastly for the CG 21 55 if unable to negotiate the 21 65. Although still saddled with an exclusion, the insured regains some protection that may prove important.

Contractual Liability Limitation

Insureds regularly enter into contractual relationships to accomplish specific business purposes. However, the unendorsed CGL policy specifically excludes liability assumed by contract (2. Exclusions: b. Contractual Liability); but the policy gives back coverage through exceptions to the exclusion.

Only one of the two exceptions to the contractual liability exclusion spell out the parameters by which contractually accepted liability is covered in the CGL. Exception (2) states that protection is provided when the following conditions are met.

- The liability is assumed by an insured contract.
- The bodily injury or property damage occurs after the execution of the contract.
- Defense and other fees are assumed in the contract (indemnify and hold harmless wording required).

- A suit alleges injury or damage covered by the policy.

(For more detail see Chapter 6: Contractual Risk Transfer Coverage Extended from the Unendorsed CGL.)

The key to the breadth of the exception is the definition of insured contract. Attachment of the **Contractual Liability Limitation** (CG 21 39) exclusionary endorsement alters the definition of insured contract by removing the all other business-related contracts provision provided by definition "f."

CG 21 39 should be avoided if at all possible. All protection normally available for and extended to many contractually created indemnitees is deleted by attachment of this exclusion. The list of contracts under which the insured can accept contractually transferred liability is limited to a short schedule which includes lease agreements, sidetrack agreements, easement or license agreements, obligations to indemnify a municipality, and an elevator maintenance agreement. No other contracts are covered as insured contracts when the **Contractual Liability Limitation** (CG 21 39) endorsement is attached.

Altering the definition of insured contract by attachment of the CG 21 39 requires the insured to make adjustments to the policy anytime it enters into a contract or agreement not contemplated in the remaining short list of acceptable contracts—provided the insured is aware of the need. The exclusion may lead to the requirement to attach additional insured endorsements, even though not requested, to meet specific contractual provisions and avoid a breach of contract or, worse, an uncovered claim.

One reason an underwriter may choose to use this drastic exclusion is the breadth of coverage extended to the indemnitee under the contractual liability exception. The sole negligence of the indemnitee (transferor) can be picked up under the unaltered wording, making the coverage granted by the unendorsed policy broader than coverage granted by most additional insured endorsements.

Agents should recommend an alternative endorsement to the underwriter wanting to avoid the unknown breadth of protection being accepted in business contracts (normally covered under "f."). The **Amendment of Insured Contract** (CG 24 26) endorsement redefines the meaning of insured contract to match the coverage granted by most additional insured endorsements. The CG 24 26 adds "... *provided the 'bodily injury' or 'property damage' is caused, in whole or in part, by you or by those acting on your behalf*" to the all other business contract wording provided in "f.", thus requiring the insured be at least partially responsible for causing the injury or damage before coverage extends to the contractual indemnitee.

Avoid the **Contractual Liability Limitation** (CG 21 39) endorsement when possible. Its presence as part of the policy requires other endorsements (an additional insured endorsement in particular) be attached to meet contractual guidelines. If the underwriter wants some control, offer the

Amendment of Insured Contract (CG 24 26) endorsement as an alternative.

Limitation of Coverage to Designated Premises or Projects

As the name suggests, the **Limitation of Coverage to Designated Premises or Projects** (CG 21 44) endorsement extends liability protection to only the location or project listed. The gap created by this endorsement is obvious. If the location or project is not specifically listed, there is no coverage.

Insureds that have a location or conduct any business, activity, or operation away from the stated premises or project may have an uncovered exposure. If this endorsement is present and an off-premises event is held, there is no coverage, unless it can be proven the other location was necessarily incidental to the listed location. Additionally, there is no coverage for a new location until the insurer is notified and the location is added (potentially negating the policy's newly acquired wording).

This exclusion is most often seen where the insured is real-estate-based and location-specific. Examples include condominium associations or apartments. But its use is not limited to these risks; in fact it can be found attached to a number of different types of risk. Nonprofit organizations seem to be particularly subject to this limitation.

Unfortunately, there is no alternative to this endorsement that can be offered to the underwriter. Anytime an agent is faced with this exclusion, he should make every effort to have the exclusion removed to avoid a possible gap.

Conclusion

Not only is knowledge of additional coverage endorsements necessary for agents to win or keep accounts, knowing what exclusionary endorsements to guard against is also beneficial. The above is not an all-inclusive list of the exclusions for which agents should be on the lookout; but they are some of the more commonly found dangerous exclusions.

Chapter 8

Ordinance or Law Coverage for Commercial Property Risks

Few commercial structures fully meet the applicable jurisdictional building codes and regulations to which they are subject. Federal, state, and local building codes are routinely reviewed, revised and updated, usually the result of newly developed technology or advances in construction methodologies or materials. Broad, sweeping revisions are most often in response to a large-scale tragedy that resulted in a large amount of property damage, a massive amount of injuries, and/or the loss of many lives. Some codes exist and change simply because of jurisdictional preference necessitated by the scarcity of some natural resources (such as water usage control requirements) or due to increased hazards faced in that locale (wind load and "earthquake proof" building requirements are examples).

Regardless of the source (federal, state or local) or the reason, all structures must be constructed to meet the building codes in force at the time of construction.

Without being too philosophical, the present becomes the past very quickly. The building that was in "perfect" compliance when built may now be noncompliant in several aspects of its design and construction. The time required to move from "in" to "out" of compliance can range from only a few months to several years depending on the frequency and nature of changes to local ordinances or laws.

Noncompliance has the potential to cost a building owner many thousands of dollars in out-of-pocket expenses following a "major" (defined later) property loss. Ordinance or law coverages are designed to fill coverage gaps existing in the unendorsed commercial property policies and business income forms related to the additional costs and time associated with the enforcement of changes in local building codes.

This chapter covers five topics related to the need for and the coverage provided by the two ordinance or law endorsements.

- Exclusionary wording within the underlying property policies which necessitates ordinance or law endorsements.
- Who promulgates the building codes affecting commercial structures.
- When a damaged structure must be brought into compliance.
- The two ordinance or law endorsements.
- How to develop coverage limits for each coverage part.

While the concepts presented in this chapter apply to virtually any commercial property policy or ordinance or law endorsement, this chapter refers to and makes use of the relevant ISO forms and endorsements in the presentation of coverage.

Coverage Gaps

Exclusions within insurance policies exist for one of six reasons. One is directly applicable to the ordinance or law exclusions. The insurance company wants more information and more money before agreeing to provide the coverage.

All three commercial property causes of loss forms (basic, broad, and special) specifically exclude the increased cost of rebuilding, repair, or remodeling created by the application of an adverse building code. Likewise, the business income policy specifically excludes any increased loss of business income (as defined in the policy) resulting from the lengthened period of restoration due to construction delays brought about by the enforcement of such codes.

Unendorsed commercial property policies pay only to replace, with building materials of like kind and quality, what existed just prior to the loss. Further, these policies only pay for the part of the structure actually damaged—even when the jurisdictional authorities do not allow the undamaged part of the structure to remain and instead require it be torn down and rebuilt.

Likewise, the unendorsed business income policy pays only for the loss of income up to the point in time when the building should have been returned to operational capability, absent any time extension directly related to the application of building codes. The period of restoration could be greatly increased as a result of and enforcement of building codes.

As is probably already evident, there is a high potential for un- insured, out-of-pocket building loss and additional loss of income when a structure suffering "major" damage (defined below) is not in substantial compliance with the applicable building codes. These additional expenses and loss of income have the potential to bankrupt a business, or at least cause devastating financial hardships.

Building Codes Created by Hundreds of Organizations

Although local jurisdictions are charged with enforcing building codes, few ordinances are actually promulgated by the enforcing body. Most building codes are adopted from modifications to model codes developed by the International Building Code Council, the federal government, and various other advisory organizations.

A state may occasionally amend a model code to strengthen particular requirements necessary to meet needs unique to them. Local jurisdictions also have the authority to alter any code to customize it to fit local needs.

One "advisory-only" federal code requires jurisdictional management and adaptation to produce a jurisdictionally-specific code: flood plain management codes. The federal government developed, maintains, and updates the initial sample guidelines, but the authority having jurisdiction must modify the program and develop its own flood plain management plan based on the locale's topography, water sources, development plans, history, and any other factors unique to the community. This is a requirement placed on any community desiring to participate in the National Flood Insurance Program (NFIP).

Other well-known construction codes emanating from the federal government include the requirements contained in the Americans with Disabilities Act (ADA) and the National Earthquake Hazard Reduction Program's (NEHRP's) model code detailing building methods designed to protect against earthquake damage in the various seismic zones.

Most building code standards, however, are developed and published by advisory organizations. A 1996 study by the National Institute of Standards and Technology (NIST) revealed that there are 93,000 standards put forth by nearly 700 distinct organizations (NIST Special Publication 806, Standards Activities of Organizations in the United States). These promulgated standards apply to all aspects of construction and building materials from acoustical tile to boilers to fire protection systems. The best known of these advisory organizations is the National Fire Protection Association (NFPA). The NFPA maintains the National Electric Code, the Life Safety Code, and essentially all advisory codes related to fire protection.

In addition to all of the above sources of construction-regulating building codes, there is a pseudo-governmental group of organizations very rarely considered when planning ordinance or law coverage: historical societies. Historical societies do not have governmental authority, per se; but they do lobby for and are granted the force of law through local ordinances governing the areas over which they have dominion (historic districts or individual historic buildings). There are currently over 85,000 sites on the National Register of

Historic Places. This does not include structures governed by state and local historical societies.

Structures guarded by an historical society may cost exponentially more to rebuild than a comparable building using modern building materials. Additionally, these structures will likely take longer to rebuild due to the lack of available period-specific materials that may be required by the governing historical society. The additional cost of and additional time required to restore a structure under the protection of an historical society must be adequately planned for when structuring and choosing ordinance or law coverage limits.

In addition, volumes of building codes may apply to a particular structure following major damage. Knowing this, it becomes quite evident that ordinance or law coverage is actually very broad in its application and payment of benefits; the only requirement is that the peril triggering the coverage be a covered cause of loss. All building codes directly controlling the rebuilding of the structure fall under the ordinance or law coverage blanket.

Multiple Definitions of "Major" Damage Creates Problems for Ordinance or Law Coverage

"Major" damage (or loss) is not necessarily a defined term in local building codes. It's simply the term chosen in this chapter to best represent the point at which the local jurisdiction considers a structure beyond safe repair due to age, condition, or previous compliance or noncompliance with building codes. This is the point at which the jurisdiction requires the entire structure be brought into compliance with current ordinances or laws.

Governing jurisdictions utilize state laws to decide when the point of "major" damage has been breached. Two of the most commonly used statutory guidelines for determining "major" damage are:

1. **The Percentage Rule**: Simply, this rule states that if the subject building is damaged beyond a set percentage of its value, the entire structure must be brought into compliance with the current building code. This percentage varies by state ranging from a low of 30 percent to as high as 60 percent.

2. **Jurisdictional Authority Rule**: Some state laws allow the authority having jurisdiction to decide at what point a structure has experience "major" damage. This could be at 40, 50, or 60 percent of its value; or it could be based solely on safety, age, or zoning conditions. Several variations of this rule are used.

Of these two disparate statutes, the Percentage Rule would seem to be the easier to understand, plan for, and apply; but it's not. The definition of value differs among the states and even jurisdictions subscribing to this rule. It may mean replacement cost, actual cash value, or appraised value; it could even be the tax value. Some states and even the federal government, in the flood policy, use market value (what a willing buyer will pay a willing seller) as the basis of value. Still other states reference the "Building Valuation Data" manual published by the International Conference of Building Officials as the source for values.

Jurisdictional Authority states introduce the problem of subjective opinion ("the rule of the person with the clipboard") into the application of local building codes. This fact makes planning very difficult, especially for insureds with buildings in multiple jurisdictions in the same state. One local authority may choose to apply a percentage-type approach, while another may be far less objective in their decision process – making it a true guess as to the outcome. States generally do not intercede in the application of the jurisdictional authority rule, making uniformity among local municipalities less likely.

Between the two, the Jurisdictional Authority Rule greatly increases the necessity of an inflation factor when calculating the amount of ordinance or law coverage to purchase. As will be seen, there is no completely reliable method to arrive at limits, but it becomes an even more haphazard process when the definition of major damage is potentially a moving target.

Complicating the application of these different rules is the situation where a building is located in a Special Flood Hazard Area (SFHA) (flood zones "A" or "V") of a Jurisdictional Authority state. Buildings located in SFHAs that suffer "substantial damage" must be brought into compliance with current flood plain management requirements as per 44CFR 59.1. The federal government defines the term "substantial damage" to mean "damaged beyond 50% of its market value."

Which rule takes precedence following a loss? Likely, the most stringent requirement shall be applied to the damaged structure. For example, the authority having jurisdiction may use and apply a rule that requires a building to be rebuilt if it is damaged beyond 50 percent of its replacement cost (RC), but the flood plain management rules require the building to be brought into flood plain management requirements when it is damaged beyond 50 percent of its market value. If the value of the damage is 35 percent of its RC, but 55 percent of its market value, then the entire building must be brought into compliance with all codes. The reverse is also true; if the local code is somehow more stringent than the flood plain management code, then the structure must be brought into full compliance following a loss that triggers the local definition of major damage.

Major damage carries a wide variety of meanings across the country depending on the state and the attitudes of the local jurisdictions. Add the federal government's superimposed authority when a structure is governed by flood plain management requirements, and the need to understand and apply ordinance or law coverage becomes more apparent.

Without one common rule or even a consistent application among the jurisdictions subscribing to essentially the same rule, it is imperative that brokers, risk managers, and/or building owners know the rules of the state or states in which properties are located, understand how major damage is defined within that rule, be aware of jurisdictional differences of opinion and be mindful of the application of flood plain management requirements. Note that the rates for ordinance or law coverage don't depend on the application of the law, but the limits purchased do.

Ordinance or Law Limitations Don't Hurt Breadth of Protection

Two primary commercial ordinance or law endorsements exist within ISO's arsenal of property forms: **Ordinance or Law Coverage** (CP 04 05) and **Ordinance or Law— Increased Period of Restoration** (CP 15 31). There also exists a Business Owners' Policy (BOP) endorsement, the BP 04 06, that is essentially the combination of the two commercial property forms. Proprietary company forms exist in the marketplace, but this discussion focuses on the ISO forms. However, the concepts discussed should apply to non-ISO forms as well.

Understanding what triggers ordinance or law coverage is paramount. Ordinance or law protection responds only if: the loss is caused by a covered peril (regardless of the form used); the loss breaches the major damage threshold as defined and applied by the subject jurisdiction; and the damaged structure is lacking in some aspect of the local building code in effect at the time of the loss.

Any loss satisfying all three triggers activates the ordinance or law coverage. However, two coverage-limiting provisions require explanation before moving to the descriptions of the three coverage parts.

1. The endorsements will pay only to the point necessary to meet the minimum code requirements applicable to the structure. Any

costs associated with going over and above the minimum code are borne by the insured. If, for example, the insured is not required by the building code to install a sprinkler system, but does anyway, the additional cost of the system is not covered by the ordinance or law endorsement because the insured is not installing it to meet code.

2. Any costs to meet codes that were required to be met prior to the loss, but weren't, are borne solely by the insured. For example, if the insured was directed by the jurisdiction to install a sprinkler system before the loss but didn't, the policy won't pay for its installation after the loss. This would violate indemnification since this is an expense the insured should have had before the loss.

Ordinance or Law Coverage (CP 04 05)

Ordinance or Law Coverage (CP 04 05) provides three distinct coverages:

- Coverage A – Coverage for Loss to the Undamaged Portion of the Building

- Coverage B – Demolition Cost Coverage

- Coverage C – Increased Cost of Construction

Coverage A – Coverage for Loss to the Undamaged Portion of the Building

Coverage A responds when a major loss triggers the application of the local ordinance or law, yet part of the building is undamaged. Essentially, the actual loss in such a claim is not just the value of the damage, but the value of the entire structure since the remaining structure has been rendered unusable by application of the local building code.

Coverage A's payment following a major damage loss relates directly to the policy limit of the underlying property policy. In essence, the maximum the insured can be paid is the total limit of coverage listed in the commercial property policy. The ultimate amount paid is a function of: the location jurisdiction's rule of major damage, the actual amount of damage, and the insured value of the building. Following is a simplified example of the application of this limit rule.

Replacement Cost at the time of loss:	$500,000 (Assume the structure is insured to value and ignore coinsurance)
Rule of Ordinance or Law:	Percentage Rule (50% of Market Value)
Amount of Damage:	$300,000
Amount Paid by Coverage A:	$200,000

In the example, the rule of law is based on market value, not on replacement cost or actual cash value (concepts common to property insurance). If the building's market value were $400,000, it is possible that a $200,000 loss could trigger the ordinance or law coverage. In such a situation, Ordinance or Law's Coverage Part A would pay $300,000. Why? The policy in this example is written on a "Replacement Cost" basis, thus the loss is settled on that basis regardless of the market value of the structure. Market value has no other concept within insurance except to trigger the ordinance or law coverage in jurisdictions that apply this guideline.

Replacement cost is placed is placed in quotation marks in the above paragraph to indicate the difference between the actual definition and application as it relates to insurance coverage, and the insured's understanding and belief of what the term means.

Coverage A follows the underlying commercial property policy lead regarding the payment on a replacement cost basis or an actual cash value basis. Additionally, the coinsurance provision in the underlying property policy applies to ordinance or law as well since any loss triggering coverage, in effect, results in a total loss.

When the replacement cost option applies, the commercial property policy combined with the ordinance or law Coverage Part A pays the lesser of:

- The amount actually spent to repair, rebuild, or reconstruct the building to the same height, floor area, style, and com- parable quality.
- The limit of insurance.

These payment options apply whether the building is rebuilt on the same or another premises. However, if the building is constructed on another premises, the policy limits the payment to what it would cost on the original premises.

Coverage A and the commercial property policy combine to pay the lesser of actual cash value or the limit of insurance if the structure is insured on an actual cash value basis or is not repaired or replaced.

A schedule of the specific locations to which this coverage part applies must be provided because Coverage A cannot be written on a blanket basis. This is the only one of the three ordinance or law coverage parts which does not have a blanket limit option.

Premium for this coverage part is a percentage of the building premium. The additional premium is approximately 15 percent of the net building premium excluding earthquake.

Coverage B – Demolition Cost Coverage

Coverage B fills the gap created by and between the commercial property policy and Coverages A and C of the Ordinance or Law coverage. Specifically, Coverage B pays the cost to demolish the undamaged portion of the partially damaged structure and remove it from the premises.

When a major loss occurs, the commercial property policy and Coverages A and B of the Ordinance or Law Coverage endorsement apply concurrently as illustrated below to ready the site for the replacement structure.

Commercial Property Policy (CPP) pays:

- The value of the actual damage to the insured structure
- The cost to remove the debris of the damaged structure

Ordinance or Law – Coverage A pays:

- The value of the undamaged part of the structure rendered unusable and valueless by the application of any ordinance or law

Ordinance or Law – Coverage B pays:

- The cost to tear down the undamaged part of the structure
- The cost to clear the site of the debris resulting from demolition of the undamaged part

Once the site is clear, construction on the new structure can begin.

Coverage B's limits are chosen by the insured and are available on a scheduled (per building) basis or blanket (one limit for all buildings) basis. Blanket limits can apply to Coverage B alone or Coverages B and C can be combined into a single blanket limit encompassing all insured locations. The last blanket limit option is a combination of scheduled coverage and blanket limit allowing the insured to purchase a combined (blanket) Coverage B and Coverage C limit but apply it to scheduled locations only. This option requires the insured to complete the Statement of Values endorsement (CP 16 15) indicating which locations are to have this coverage. Coinsurance requirements do not apply to Coverage B.

Calculating the Coverage B premium is simple. The additional premium is developed by dividing the chosen Coverage B limit by 100 and multiplying that quotient by the net building rate at what- ever coinsurance limit is being used. The net rate used should not include agreed value or inflation guard factors.

Coverage C – Increased Cost of Construction

This third leg of ordinance or law coverage represents and provides the funds necessary to pay the difference between the re- placement cost as defined in the insurance policy and the insured's belief about and understanding of its meaning. In short, Coverage C pays the costs in excess of the amount paid by the underlying commercial property policy necessary to bring the damaged structure into compliance with the building code in effect at the time of loss. Without Coverage C, the insured would have to pay these additional building costs out-of-pocket.

Coverage C has the added benefit of extending protection for some classes of real property specifically excluded in the commercial property policy. Losses triggering the enforcement of the local building code trigger Coverage C to add the cost of excavations, grading, backfilling and filling, building foundations, pilings and underground pipes, flues and drains to the list of insured property. Further, it is possible to have an ordinance or law claim and payment under Coverage C only. The last of the three covered losses allows payment under

Coverage C without the need for payout under Coverages A or B. The three types of losses to which Coverage C responds are:

- The cost to repair or reconstruct the damaged portion of the building.
- The cost to reconstruct the undamaged portion of the building if demolition is required.
- The cost to remodel the undamaged portion of the building if demolition is not required.

Three caveats must be satisfied before Coverage C applies.

1. The rebuilt or remodeled property must be intended for similar occupancy (unless such occupancy is no longer permitted).

2. To receive payment under Coverage C, the building must first be rebuilt or remodeled. There is no option to take the actual cash value (ACV) of the upgrades in the commercial property policy and Coverage A. If the insured decides to not rebuild, the insured will receive the ACV of the damaged part of the building from the commercial property policy plus the ACV of the undamaged portion of the building will be paid under Coverage A.

3. Repairs or replacement must be made as soon as reasonably possible, but they must be completed within two years after the loss. If it appears that more than two years will be required, the

insured can request an extension. The insurer will evaluate the request based on the conditions surrounding the request and may or may not grant the extension.

The insured can choose to rebuild anywhere; but the most Coverage C will pay (subject to the limit of insurance purchased) is the increased amount necessary to replace the building at the insured premises. If, however, the local ordinance or law requires the building be relocated, then this coverage part will pay the lesser of the increased cost at the new premises or the limit of coverage.

Since the goal of Coverage C is to replace the damaged building with an improved one, the underlying property coverage must be written on a replacement cost basis, preferably insured at or near 100 percent of insurance-to-value (ITV). Doing so will remove most limit gaps and coinsurance problems. Notice, however, that the coinsurance condition does not apply to Coverage C.

Coverage C coverage options mirror those available to Coverage B:

- Scheduled locations and limits
- Blanket Coverage C limit applying to all insured locations
- Blanket combined Coverage B and Coverage C limit applying to all locations

- Combined Coverage B and Coverage C limit applying to specific locations (requires the **Statement of Values** form CP 16 15)

Likewise, premium development for Coverage C is the same as for Coverage B. The chosen Coverage C limit is divided by 100 and multiplied by the net building rate at whatever coinsurance limit is being used. The net rate used should not include agreed value or inflation guard factors.

In 2017, ISO published an updated edition of this endorsement. This update provided one very interesting expansion of coverage. There is now a check box on the first page which simply reads "Post-Loss Ordinance Or Law Option" with two options, yes or no.

This option allows for coverage to apply if a new ordinance or law is passed after the loss occurs, but before repairs are started. It is also necessary that the new law require that the insured comply with it before they can receive a building permit or certificate of occupancy. This is a limited expansion of coverage for some very specific situations.

Ordinance or Law – Increased Period of Restoration (CP 15 31)

As its name suggests, this endorsement redefines the Business Income Policy's definition of period of restoration to include any increase in such period resulting from the application of any ordinance or law. Simply stated, if the building code lengthens the period of restoration, the income lost during this extended period is included in the definition of business income. Without this endorsement, income lost during this extended period is paid out of the insured's pocket.

But this one change provides a potentially huge benefit to the insured. Period of restoration in the unendorsed Business Income Policy is defined as the time period beginning 72 hours (or whatever amount of time is negotiated) after the loss and ending the earlier of the date business is resumed at a different location; or the date the property at the described premises should be repaired, rebuilt, or replaced with reasonable speed and similar quality. Any delay arising out of the application of any ordinance or law that increases this period, resulting in additional loss of income, is specifically excluded in the policy.

The **Ordinance or Law – Increased Period of Restoration** (CP 15 31) endorsement redefines the period of restoration to include any increase in time necessary to repair or reconstruct the property as a result of the application of any building code. As in the **Ordinance or Law Coverage** (CP 04 05) endorsement, the building code(s) causing this increase in time must be in effect at the time of the loss, unless the post-loss ordinance or law option is selected. CP 15 31 could be the more important of the two ordinance or law endorsements.

Most businesses cannot operate, at least not for very long, unless there is a stream of income. Rarely does a business close (or fail to reopen) after a major loss due to inadequate property coverage. Even if the property coverage is inadequate, alternative financing sources can be found to assist in rebuilding the structure. Businesses that fail to reopen after a major property loss or close shortly after reopening do so because of the crippling loss of and lack of income.

Accurately anticipating the additional period of restoration resulting from the application of local building codes is, at best, a guess. Some of the time factors unique to ordinance or law which must be considered are listed below.

- Time necessary for the authority having jurisdiction to decide if the building has breached the major damage trigger. This period can vary greatly among jurisdictions depending on the rule and guidelines applied.

- Time necessary for the jurisdiction to decide if the building must be torn down or can be remodeled.

- Time to find and schedule a demolition contractor.

- Time required to clear and re-grade the site after demolition.

- Time to draw new plans.

- Time to get the plans approved.

- Time to rebuild the building code.

Individually or combined, the time factors listed above (and others not on the list) could easily morph into several weeks or months. Without the CP 15 31, the insured would have no coverage for the income lost during the additional period of restoration attributable to the application of any ordinance or law.

Adding the CP 15 31 to the business income coverage increases the time element premium approximately 20 percent (more if earthquake coverage is included). Compared to the catastrophic consequences of not purchasing the coverage, this is a very reasonable premium.

Neither the **Ordinance or Law** (CP 04 05) nor the **Ordinance or Law—Increased Period of Restoration** (CP 15 31) endorsements pay for loss caused by or due to contamination by pollutants or the presence, growth, proliferation, spread, or any activity of fungus, wet or dry rot, or bacteria; or the additional cost or time to test for, monitor, clean up, remove, treat detoxify, or neutralize the effects of pollutants, etc.

How to Calculate the Correct Amount of Ordinance or Law Coverage

The fifth topic mentioned at beginning of this chapter pertains to how coverage limits are chosen. The next several paragraphs provide some guidance in this process.

Coverage A – Coverage for Loss to the Undamaged Portion of the Building

Coverage A does not require a limit be chosen. The endorsement pays the difference between the value of the damaged part of the property and the total building limit specified in the commercial property policy.

The real decision is made when the underlying commercial property limit is calculated. If the building limit chosen is too low, the combination of the commercial property limit and Coverage A will likewise be too low and may be subject to the coinsurance penalty.

Providing 100 percent insurance-to-value (ITV) ensures the best opportunity to have adequate combined coverage. Using a reliable replacement cost estimator program coupled with knowledge of the local building trends are the best markers when choosing the initial limits of coverage.

Coverage B – Demolition Cost Coverage

What will it cost to tear down and remove the undamaged portion of the structure? The answer will depend on circumstances surrounding the loss and the characteristics of the structure, including:

- What does it cost within the local construction market to demolish a building and remove it from the site?
- How much of the building is not damaged?
- At what point will the jurisdictional authorities require the building to be torn down?
- Are there any special hazard issues such as asbestos, mold, etc.?

Determining the cost to tear down and remove the undamaged portion of the structure is as much an art as a science. The result is little more than an educated guess based on the answers to these questions and other circumstances particular to a specific structure. Purely for example sake and not intended as a recommendation or rule, Exhibit 8.1 at the end of this chapter provides a fictitious loss scenario toward developing Coverage B limits. Alter any or several factors in the exhibit, and the amount of required Coverage B changes.

Lacking any other plan or method, consider the following four- step process for calculating the amount of Coverage B to purchase.

1. Determine the worst case scenario. This is the minimum amount of loss necessary to trigger the application of the local building codes.

2. Convert the worst-case scenario amount into square footage. This conversion may not be exact, but it is necessary to calculate a limit.

3. Contact several local building and demolition contractors to develop an average cost per square foot for demolition and removal.

4. Multiply the square footage developed in step 2 by the average cost per square foot for demolition and removal.

There is no guarantee that this will generate the exact amount needed, but it should be relatively close to the limit needed for almost any loss.

Coinsurance does not apply to Coverage B and blanket limits are available. Make use of these coverage part advantages where possible.

Coverage C – Increased Cost of Construction

Of the three coverage parts, choosing a limit for the increased cost of construction may be the most difficult to calculate. This chapter has touched on the difference between the true meaning of replacement cost within the insurance contract and the insured's understanding of and expectations of replacement cost. Coverage C is intended to provide the funds to finance the gap between reality and belief.

Perhaps the insurance industry is to blame for the gap between reality and belief, the origins of which are found in a misunderstanding of replacement cost. In fact, the industry is probably almost totally to blame due to the continued misrepresentation of the definition. Insureds are routinely told that replacement cost means new for old, either directly or by implication. It is common for insureds to hear "Your building is insured for replacement cost. If it burns down, the insurance company will pay to build you a new building." This over-simplified definition of replacement cost is promulgated over and over.

Furthermore, an agent or broker sometimes doesn't know the application of the true definition or doesn't want to complicate the conversation by providing the definition and the applicable caveats, particularly that the unendorsed policy will only pay to replace what was there just prior to the loss, not any additional features required by building codes. There are times, though, when the agent/ broker does detail this information to the insured, but the insured does not pay attention or does not remember the conversation. The insured hears what he wants to hear, and he may create expectations of coverage based on what he believes he heard.

Where Coverage B involved an educated guess, Coverage C is devoid of any readily apparent avenues of educated information. Most replacement cost estimators develop and present the cost per square foot necessary to rebuild the building to current building code, with no method of deduction for its current out-of-code status. Further, the age of the building is not a reliable indicator as there may have been updates at different times throughout the years. To complicate matters further, it is not likely that any builder or contractor can provide an accurate estimate of what it might cost to rebuild the structure as it exists since all their cost estimators, like replacement cost estimators, are based on current codes. Lastly, with the time value of money and improvements in construction methods and materials, using old estimators and adjusting them to current values will not provide an accurate estimate.

Ultimately, the limit chosen will be based on little more than a guess. One suggested method may be to assign a percentage of the building value and multiply that value by the age of the building. Some application or derivative of this methodology may provide the most explainable and defensible Coverage C calculation. Applying the same percentage to each year allows the ultimate percentage to account for fluctuations among the years regarding code changes. Some years may have seen major code changes, with other years experiencing no code changes. This is akin to dollar cost averaging in financial planning.

For example, assume a chosen percentage of 1 percent per year on a 10-year-old building. Applying the cost averaging method to a $500,000 building would produce a Coverage C limit of $50,000. Structures facing unique hazards, such as being located in a Special Flood Hazard Area (SFHA), may need to adjust the limit/percentage to respond to the extra hazard.

Coinsurance does not apply to Coverage C, so there is no requirement to pick the exact limit. The goal is to mitigate, as fully as possible, the cost to the insured of bringing the building into compliance with the current building code following a major loss. For ease and to increase the chance of having an adequate amount of coverage, there is an option to purchase blanket Coverage C limits.

Coverage A does not require a limit choice as part of the endorsement; the choice is made in the underlying property policy. Coverage B is a somewhat educated guess. And Coverage C may be best described as a guess of irreducible complexity.

Ordinance or Law Coverage Claim Example

Explaining the need for Ordinance or Law coverage and selling the insured on paying the additional premium may necessitate presenting a realistic claim example. Exhibit 8.2 at the end of the chapter illustrates the same loss but with two potential outcomes; one if both ordinance or law endorsements apply and second, the possible outcome when only the commercial property policy and unendorsed business income coverage is used. For sake of the example, assume the building is correctly and fully insured and ignore any deductibles.

This example presents a very realistic claim scenario. With both ordinance or law endorsements in use, the insured is fully insured. Conversely, without the endorsements, the insured will be out of pocket $3,825,000 in actual costs and loss of income. By increasing their property premium by about 30 percent (that adds about $7,500 on a $25,000 property premium), the insured could have purchased the necessary additional limits.

One possible claim scenario yet to be discussed involves multiple causes of loss where some perils are covered by the underlying commercial property policy and some portion of the loss is excluded from the CPP's coverage. The best example is the combination of wind and flood damage. In combined-loss situations such as this, the Ordinance or Law Coverage will pay pro-rata based on the percentage of damaged caused by each peril (once the court decides what that percentage is). If the wind causes 40 percent of the damage and the flood the other 60 percent, the Ordinance or Law Coverage will pay 40 percent of the loss in all three coverage parts.

Conclusion

Structures more than five years old are likely deficient in some aspect of applicable building codes. **Ordinance or Law Coverage** (CP 04 05) and **Ordinance or Law—Increased Period of Restoration** (CP 15 31) are very broad forms designed to financially address these deficiencies. Purchased together, these endorsements pay the additional costs and loss of income resulting from the application of any ordinance or law affecting the reconstruction of the covered structure.

Since building codes have the potential to change rapidly, not all jurisdictions apply the same rules of what constitutes major damage, gaps exist in the coverage provided by the commercial property policy (CPP) and the actual application of replacement cost is not completely understood or explained, these two endorsements could literally be the difference between the insured's ability to reopen following a major property loss and the business becoming a statistic.

Key Questions

- How old is the structure?
- When were the last major updates?
- What rule of major damage is applied by the jurisdiction?
- Is the structure located in a Special Flood Hazard Area (SFHA)?
- Is the structure under the protection of any historical society?

Example 8.1 Demolition Calculation

Building Square Footage: 25,000

Replacement Cost: $2,500,000

Market Value: $1,800,000

Jurisdictional Law: 50% of **market value**

Loss Value: $1,000,000

Square Footage Damaged: 15,000

Square Footage
Undamaged: 10,000

Cost to Demolish & Remove: $5.00 per square foot

Coverage B would need to be at least $50,000 to pay for the demolition and removal of the undamaged building in this example.

Example 8.2 – Claim Comparison

Building Information and Loss Factors

Total Building Value:	$2,500,000	Age of Building:	30 years old
12-month Business Income:	$3,500,000	Occupancy	Manufacturing
Value of Loss:	$1,300,000	Building Square Footage:	25,000
Estimated BI Loss:	$2,450,000 (70% coinsurance)	Sq. Foot of Damage:	13,000
		Sq. Foot Undamaged:	12,000
Actual BI Loss due to application of building code:	$3,500,000	Estimated Period of Restoration:	8 Months
Jurisdictional Law:	50% of Value	Actual Period of Restoration (due to ord. or law):	12 Months

Ordinance or Law Coverage

Coverage A - Included in CPP

Coverage B - $60,000

Coverage C - $350,000

Includes **Increased Period of Restoration** Endorsement

Claim Payment Comparison:

Loss Type	Actual Loss	Paid w/ CPP and both Ordinance or Law Endorsements	Paid using unendorsed CPP and BI Only
Building Damage:	$1,300,000	$1,300,000	$1,300,000
Business Income: (1)	$3,500,000	$3,500,000	$2,450,000
Value of Undamaged Portion: (2)	$1,200,000	$1,200,000	0
Demolition Cost Total: (3)	$125,000	$125,000	$65,000
Increased Cost of Construction:	$300,000	$300,000	$10,000
Total	**$6,425,000**	**$6,425,000**	**$3,825,00**

o

(1) Period of Restoration is 12 months as a result of additional time required to comply with the local building codes. Without the application of building codes, the period of restoration would have been 8 months.

(2) Remaining structure must be torn down due to the local building code requirements.

(3) Total cost of demolition and removal includes damaged and undamaged parts of the building at $5.00 per square foot.

Chapter 9

Understanding Personal Lines Ordinance or Law Protection

Exponential technological advances, improvements in building materials and methods, changes in external and environmental conditions, and the rewriting and recodification of building codes all occur during the lifespan of a typical house. The result, within 10 years of completion (maybe even as little as 5 years), the house may violate some part of the most current jurisdictional building codes.

Any house not in compliance with current building codes subjects the owners to a coverage limit gap following a major loss (as defined in chapter 8) because specific jurisdictional requirements stipulate the point at which a particular house has suffered major damage and must be brought into building code compliance; and ISO's unendorsed homeowners' policy provides only a minimal amount of coverage to pay for the increased expenses resulting from the enforcement of current building codes. Combined, the limitations on coverage and the building code's specifications can lead to a potentially large out-of-pocket expense for the insured.

Major Damage Rules

Major loss or damage is uniquely defined by individual jurisdictions with each applying its own connotative twist. Most state and local building codes fall into two broad categories of rules.

1. **The Jurisdictional Authority Rule**: States applying this as the measure of major damage allow the authority having jurisdiction (the local government) to judge when a damaged building must be brought in its entirety into compliance with the current building code.

2. **The Percentage Rule**: Simply, when a building is damaged beyond a certain percentage of its value, the entire structure must be brought into compliance with local building code. There is no subjective interpretation involved.

Each rule presents its own set of problems regarding ordinance or law coverage and the minimal limits automatically provided in most homeowners' policies.

- The **Jurisdictional Authority Rule** is subjective in its application. Each jurisdiction develops and applies its own standard to define major damage and determine a structure's fitness for continued use. Decisions can be based on the amount of damage, the age of the building coupled with pre-loss compliance shortfalls, or simple safety concerns. There is no one criteria upon which homeowners and their agents can depend, making risk management and insurance planning very difficult in states applying this rule. The jurisdictional authority rule has been likened to being "at the mercy of the man with the clipboard."

- The **Percentage Rule's** definition of value differs among the states applying this as their codified statute. Value in these states could mean anything from actual cash value to appraised value or even market value. Such breadth of interpretation can create problems for agents that operate in more than one state.

Ordinance or Law Sources

Building ordinances and laws enforced by local jurisdictions are promulgated by a wide assortment of contributors. States use these model codes to create a statutory infrastructure but endow to local jurisdictions the authority to adopt and customize building codes to meet local preferences and needs as necessary. Building codes and ordinances are developed and published by the following entities.

The Federal Government

Three major advisory codes flow from the federal government: flood plain management requirements, building requirements contained in the Americans with Disabilities Act (ADA), and the National Earthquake Hazards Reduction Program (NEHRP) model code. All of these are model codes, most specifically the flood plain management requirements (communities desiring to be part of the NFIP must develop

their own code utilizing the model code from FEMA). Each
state and even the local jurisdictions mold these codes to fit
their particular need and exposure. These are not the only
codes developed by the federal government, but they are the
best known.

Advisory Organizations

Most codes and standards are developed, monitored, and
updated by independent advisory organizations. A 1996
National Institute of Standards and Technology (NIST) study
revealed that 700 distinct advisory organizations account for
more than 93,000 separate standards and codes (not all are
building codes; these include codes for materials, boilers, fire
protection systems, etc.).

State and Local Government

Each state and local jurisdiction has the authority, subject
to certain minimum requirements, to massage codes and
ordinances as necessary to meet that jurisdiction's needs.

Historical Societies

Although these societies are not branches of local, state or
national governments, they are granted pseudo-governmental
authority regarding the rebuilding of particular structures.
Historical societies' goal is to save the historical integrity of a
structure for future generations. Such efforts, while admirable,
can significantly increase the cost of rebuilding a house under
the society's control. Any house in an historical district merits

special attention and potentially special endorsements outside the intended scope of this chapter.

Agents planning their homeowner client's insurance and risk management program with these authorities and exposures in mind should have the following areas of expertise.

- A basic understanding of the building codes applicable to and affecting their homeowners' clients.
- Knowledge about which rule of major damage is applied.
- Well-versed in how the individual jurisdiction applies the specified rule.

Gaps in the Unendorsed Homeowners' Form

ISO's unendorsed Homeowners' Policy (e.g., the HO-3) provides a limited amount of coverage to pay the costs associated with the enforcement of any ordinance or law following a major loss. The following discussion gives the coverage and limit provided by the unendorsed homeowners' policy, lists the types of government-induced losses this limited amount is required to cover, and provides claims examples.

Coverage Included in the Homeowners' Policy

Unendorsed, ISO's homeowners' policies provide only 10 percent of Coverage A (Dwelling), in addition to the Coverage A limit, to pay the cost of a loss or increase in loss resulting from the enforcement of any ordinance or law to which the house is subject. For example, a policy with a $300,000 Coverage A limit would provide up to only $30,000 of additional protection to cover the added expenses arising from a building code-induced loss. Such limit would be called upon to cover three "additional costs" as detailed in the policy's Additional Coverage—Ordinance or Law provision.

- *The increased cost necessary to bring the damaged part of the house up to current code;*
- *The cost to tear down and remove the debris of the undamaged part of the structure; and*
- *The cost to rebuild or repair the undamaged part of the structure in compliance with current building code.*

That's a lot in expenses to expect from such a minimal amount of coverage. Remember, apart from this extension or any attached ordinance or law endorsement (if any), the homeowners' policy pays only the cost to tear down, remove the debris of, and rebuild/repair the damaged part of the house. No coverage other than this additional coverage applies to the undamaged part of the house.

An example using the same $300,000 house will help spotlight the potential limit gap. Following are several of the pertinent facts necessary for this example.

- Value of house: $300,000
- Square footage: 3,000
- Ordinance or Law Additional Coverage (included in the policy): $30,000

- Ordinance or Law Rule applied by the jurisdiction: Percentage Rule (60% of value)
- Amount of Damage: $200,000 (66.7%)
- Square Footage Damaged: 2,000 square feet

Based on the above information, assume the jurisdiction requires the house to be torn down and rebuilt to meet current building code. The homeowners' coverage part will only pay the $200,000 plus the cost to remove the debris of the *damaged* property. Any additional cost resulting directly from the application of one or several ordinances or laws is specifically excluded (except for the small amount granted in the additional coverages section). So, how will the coverage break down? What claims costs will the ordinance or law extension be required to cover and how much will the insured have to pay from his own pocket?

The 10% ($30,000) ordinance or law coverage will be called upon to pay the additional per-square-foot cost to bring the damaged part of the structure up to current building code once rebuilt, the cost to tear down the remaining (undamaged) part of the structure, and the cost to rebuild the undamaged part of the structure to comply with the current building code. What might all of this cost, and is $30,000 enough? We need to make some assumptions needed to complete this example.

- Cost to rebuild to current building code: $120 per sq. ft.
- Cost to rebuild to old code: $100 per sq. ft.
- Demolition and Debris Removal cost: $5.00 per sq. ft.

Using this information and the costs and limits presented above, the homeowners coupled with the ordinance or law additional coverage will respond and pay as follows:

Homeowners' Policy (without the additional coverage)

- Cost to remove the debris of the damaged portion of the house: $10,000 (2,000 sq. ft. x $5 per sq. ft.)
- Cost to rebuild the damaged portion of the house to old code: $200,000 (2,000 sq. ft. x $100 per sq. ft.)
  Total amount paid by the homeowners' coverage (without the additional ordinance or law coverage): $210,000

Additional Coverage – Ordinance or Law

- Additional cost to bring the damaged portion of the house up to current building code: $40,000 (2,000 sq. ft. x $20 per sq. ft., the difference between old building code and current building code)
- Cost to tear down and remove undamaged portion of the house: $5,000 (1,000 sq. ft. x $5 sq. ft.)
- Cost to rebuild the undamaged part of the house to current building code: $120,000 (1,000 sq. ft. x $120 per sq. ft.)
  Total amount that would be directly related to the enforcement of the ordinance or law: $165,000

The amount of coverage available in the unendorsed policy is only $30,000; so the insured in this example would be out of pocket $135,000.

Even if the above example were altered to 80% of the house being damaged, the cost to comply with local building code as per the above breakdown would still be around $123,000 ($93,000 out of the insured's pocket).

Going one step further, if the difference between the old building code and the new is only $10 per square foot, and if the house is 80% damaged, the amount provided by the ordinance or law extension is still short by $63,000 ($93,000 total cost minus the $30,000 available).

(NOTE: Contents coverage and loss of use are not considered in the cost of the above claim example.)

Total Loss

Essentially, the application of an ordinance or law requiring the house to be torn down and rebuilt to current code creates a total loss for the insured even if the house was not totally destroyed by the covered cause of loss. And the additional cost created by the enforcement of the building code is specifically excluded by the policy and coverage is limited to the amount given back in the Additional Coverage—Ordinance or Law provision (unless increased by endorsement).

Loss/Gap and the Reality of Building Codes

In all the prior examples, the greatest ordinance or law expense is the cost associated with the undamaged portion of the house (the cost to tear down and rebuild to current code).

However, consideration must be given to the fact that it is not likely a house could be 80 percent damaged and not be declared a total loss or at least a constructive total loss (unless it's a magic fire that just stops and causes no further damage). This massive cost and gap in coverage limit is most likely to be found in a house that suffers 50 to 60 percent damage.

Discounting the costs associated with the undamaged part of the house, the cost to bring the entire house up to current building code could, itself, use up and greatly exceed the ordinance or law coverage offered in the unendorsed homeowners' policy. In the first example, the cost to bring the entire house up to current code is $60,000 (3,000 square feet times $20 per square foot) leaving the homeowner out of pocket $30,000.

The difference between the cost to rebuild the structure as it stood and the cost to bring it to current building code is largely a function of the house's age and the rapidity and breadth of changes in the building codes adopted by the authority having jurisdiction. Agents should have a good handle on the major changes between the time the house was built and the current building code. Even so, it is nearly impossible to know all applicable building codes (several volumes of manuals are necessary to hold them). But the agent can undertake to know the major changes involving major requirements such as are contained in the National Electrical Code, the applicable flood plain management codes, and other major changes (such as ADA guidelines and changes in building procedures and materials) since the house was constructed.

As stated earlier, the building codes applicable to a specific house, while enforced by the local authority, can emanate from innumerable sources; but the good news is that ordinance or law coverage responds to all building codes, regardless of the genesis. The policy specifically states, *"You may use up to 10% of the limit of liability that applies to Coverage 'A' for the increased costs you incur due to the enforcement of any ordinance or law which requires or regulates...."* Any has no limitation.

Homeowners' Endorsements Not Altering the Ordinance or Law Exclusion/Limitation

Additional Limits of Liability for Coverages A, B, C and D (HO 04 11) or equivalent state-specific form) – This form allows the insured to purchase an additional amount of dwelling coverage (Coverage A) after the loss occurs in the event that the estimated replacement cost purchased was less than the actual replacement cost (the old "guaranteed replacement cost" coverage). Once additional Coverage A limits are purchased, all other coverage parts increase in kind (based on the applicable percentages), including the 10 percent additional coverage for ordinance or law.

Endorsement provisions require the insured to: carry 100% insurance-to-value, allow the insurance carrier to adjust the limits based on replacement cost valuations completed, allow the insurer to apply an inflation factor, and notify the insurance carrier if any improvements are made that increase the value of the structure more than 5 percent.

However, this endorsement does not alter the Ordinance or Law Exclusion in the loss settlement provisions. ISO's HO-3 form specifically states, *"In this Condition C., the terms 'cost to repair or replace' and 'replacement cost' do **not** include the increased costs incurred to comply with the enforcement of any ordinance or law, except to the extent that coverage for these increased costs is provided in E.11. Ordinance Or Law under Section I – Property Coverages."* (Emphasis added.) The E.11. additional coverage is the 10 percent of Coverage A as discussed previously.

Specified Additional Amount of Insurance For Coverage A – Dwelling (HO 04 20) or equivalent state-specific (form) – This is a modified version of the HO 04 11 containing all the same provisions and limitations. The major difference is that only Coverage Part A (Dwelling) can be increased. None of the other limits, including the ordinance or law limit, are increased. A second difference of this endorsement is that the amount of additional coverage available for purchase is limited to either 25 percent or 50 percent of the pre-loss Coverage A (whichever the underwriting carrier will allow).

The HO 04 20 uses the same definition of replacement cost as the HO 04 11; meaning that none of the additional costs required by the application of an ordinance or law are covered by the attachment of this endorsement.

Resulting Confusion

Confusion over both forms is generated by a misunderstanding of the meaning of replacement cost used in the homeowners' form and the subject endorsements. Replacement cost means to replace with like kind and quality. Basically this translates as to put back exactly what was there, like it was, using new material; but excluding the cost of any upgrades requested by the insured or mandated by any governmental authority.

The definition of replacement cost does not include certain costs that may be required.

- Raise the house 3 feet to get it above Base Flood Elevation (BFE) to comply with the current flood plain management code.
- Add more electrical outlets to meet National Electrical Code (NEC) Requirements.
- Move the house back 10 feet to meet set-back requirements.
- Widen doorways and raise counters to meet ADA requirements.

All of these costs result from governmental ordinances or laws and are examples of expenses not included in the definition of replacement cost. So, even buying more Coverage A will not cover these expenses. The cost to meet any or all of these and other jurisdictional requirements will have to be covered under the ordinance or law extension in the unendorsed HO policy, covered under the endorsement increasing coverage (HO 04 77), or paid out of the insured's pocket (if there is not enough additional coverage from either of the other options).

In short, neither endorsement rescues the insured from the additional costs necessitated by a local jurisdiction's enforcement of the local building codes requiring a house to be brought, in its entirety, up to current building code.

Ordinance or Law Endorsements for the Homeowners' Policy

Two ordinance or law endorsements exist for use with homeowners' policies: the **Ordinance or Law Increased Amount of Coverage** (HO 04 77) and the **Ordinance or Law Coverage** (HO 05 62). The HO 05 62 is attached when there is no automatic ordinance or law coverage provided by the homeowners' form. Coverage provided by this endorsement is the same as has been discussed previously except that the insured chooses the coverage limit desired.

However, since most ISO homeowners' policies include ordinance or law as an additional coverage, this chapter focuses on the use of the HO 04 77 to increase the amount of ordinance or law coverage.

Coverage breadth is not changed by the HO 04 77, only the amount of coverage. The insured can choose to increase the limits to 25 percent, 50 percent, 75 percent, or even 100 percent of Coverage A. The premiums for each level is a percentage of the homeowners' base premium ranging from 13 percent (to increase to 25 percent of Coverage A) up to 67 percent (raising the limit to 100 percent of Coverage A).

The first example presented earlier developed an ordinance or law-induced claim expense of $165,000; that equates to about 55 percent of Coverage A. Increasing the ordinance or law limit to 50 percent of Coverage A would increase the base premium by approximately 35 percent. A $1,000 premium would become a $1,350 premium; but that $350 is preferable to the out-of-pocket expense of $135,000 presented in the example.

But, as previously stated, such such a loss and extreme application of an ordinance or law claim is probably rare. However, it is still highly recommended and even professionally necessary to offer additional amounts of ordinance or law coverage, at least the 25 percent option. In some states, such as Florida, the agent is required to offer the 25 percent and 50 percent alternatives; and the insured has the option to purchase or reject the offer of coverage (by signature).

Conclusion

Ordinance or law coverage is more commonly discussed and highlighted in commercial property conversations, but rarely is such a discussion carried on with personal lines clients. As was presented in this chapter, the lack of this coverage has the potential to be very expensive for the insured (and potentially the agency if an errors and omissions suit results).

Not to be overly dramatic, but ordinance or law is a very real personal lines exposure often overlooked during the personal lines risk management and insurance planning process. Agents should offer the protection and explain the exposure as clearly and quickly as possible, especially to clients in a home 10 years old or older. A great marketing opportunity may be to write a letter to clients owning older homes to explain their exposure and present a solution. Regardless, agents should not ignore this potential out-of- pocket expense faced by their homeowner clients.

Exhibit 9.1 is a sample letter agents can send to homeowner clients to explain the ordinance or law coverage gap. The letter will serve two purposes: it is a marketing tool to let homeowner clients know that the agent is looking out for their best interests; and it is errors and omissions protection for the agent. If a client suffers major damage leading to an ordinance or law rebuilding requirement that is not paid by insurance, being able to prove in court that the insured had been notified of this potential gap will go a long way towards protecting the agent from an errors and omissions claim and will help win the case.

Exhibit 9.1
Ordinance or Law Letter to Homeowners

Feel free to print this letter to your letterhead, making any necessary modifications. Several parts of the letter are in parentheses, underlined, and italicized. These areas are to be filled in with specific information about the client, such as the Coverage A limit or the amount extended for Ordinance or Law coverage.

121

(Note: This letter is solely intended to assist the agent in introducing this exposure to clients and in no way guarantees that the agent will be protected from any charges related to the conduct of his/her business or operation as an agent or agency. The duty to identify and manage a client's, prospect's, or any other party's risk lies fully with the agent. Wells Media Group assumes no liability associated with the use or non-use of this letter.)

Dear (*Homeowner*),

Building codes are constantly changed and updated. Houses in total compliance just a few years ago may no longer meet your community's current building code requirements. In fact, homes built more than 10 years ago (maybe even as new as 5 or 6 years old) may not comply with today's laws and ordinances.

Any lack of compliance, although unintentional, could be personally costly following a major loss to your home. Standard, unendorsed homeowners' policies provide only a limited amount of coverage to pay for any additional cost caused by the building inspector's insistence that your entire home be brought into full compliance with local building codes following a loss.

Your homeowners' policy provides *(amount of coverage)* coverage on your home; an additional *(use 10% of the previous amount)* is available to cover the added expense necessary to comply with local building code. That *(10% amount above)* is all that is available to pay:

- The cost to tear down the undamaged portion of the house (so the entire house can be rebuilt to code).
- The cost to rebuild the entire house to current building code (the damaged and undamaged parts).

By itself, *(the 10% amount)* may not give you enough coverage to accomplish these requirements. Any amount above *(the 10% amount)* will have to be paid by *you*.

You do have the option to increase your protection and save yourself from this out-of-pocket expense. The **Ordinance or Law Increased Amount of Coverage** endorsement (HO 04 77 *(or whatever state (or carrier) specific endorsement is used)*) can be attached to fill this gaping hole. Several levels of protection are available to meet your needs.

We feel you need to be aware of your policy's current limits and coverage limitations. You also need to know that there is a way to fill the gap and protect yourself from a potentially devastating out-of-pocket expense. Please call us to explore your options.

Sincerely,

Agent's Name (Signature)

Chapter 10
Understanding Utility Service Coverage

ISO's 2007 edition of the Causes of Loss – Special Form
(CP 10 30) was approved, adopted, and fully implemented in
all states by late 2008. One result of the new causes of loss
wording was the removal of on-premises utility service
coverage from the form.

Prior editions of the Causes of Loss – Special Form (2002
and previous forms) extended coverage to include protection
against the financial consequences of property losses caused by
damage to utility service devices located *on* the insured's
premises; only utility service-related losses that originated off
the insured's premises had been excluded. But this changed
with the adoption of the 06 07 edition of the commercial
property Causes of Loss— Special Form (CP 10 30 06 07).
These changes continue with the adoption of the 2017 edition.

The commercial property Causes of Loss – Special Form
excludes damage resulting from the failure of or damage to any
utility service device, regardless of where the damage occurs
(on or off premises). In fact, five changes specific to the utility
service exclusion were made in this filing.

- The Causes of Loss – Special Form (CP 10 30),
  applicable to both property and time element
  coverages, excludes damage resulting from the failure

of on-premises equipment used to supply the utility
service from an off-premises source.

- The exclusionary wording was made identical for both
  the property coverage and the time element coverage.

- Communications and water services were specifically
  added to the list of utility services eligible for coverage.
  Previously only power was scheduled.

- Power surge is specifically excluded.

- Communication services including Internet access or
  access to cellular or satellite networks.

In part, the 06 07 edition of the utility service exclusion
reads:

e. Utility Services

*The failure of power, communication, water or other
utility service supplied to the described premises, however
caused, if the failure:*

(1) Originates away from the described premises; or

*(2) Originates at the described premises, but only if
such failure involves equipment used to supply the
utility service to the described premises from a source
away from the described premises.*

Key in this exclusionary wording is, "however caused." This means that even if the service interruption is caused by an otherwise covered cause of loss (i.e., lightning), the resulting damage attributable solely to the interruption of utility service is excluded.

Also contained in this language is an exception to the on-premises exclusion. Note that the on-premises exclusion applies only if the damaged equipment is used to supply utility service "from a source away from the described premises." Essentially, the exclusionary wording does not preclude coverage for damage resulting from damage to on-premises generators (for example). Direct property loss caused by damage to an on-premises utility service, such as a generator, is covered under this wording.

Utility Service Coverage Claim Example

Suppose a severe thunderstorm releases damaging cloud-to- ground lightning. During the storm, a transformer on the premises of a local restaurant is struck and damaged by lightning, causing the power to go out and resulting in thousands of dollars in spoiled food. Will the loss be covered in the restaurant's unendorsed property policy utilizing the 06 07 edition of the Causes of Loss – Special Form?

As per the above policy wording, the loss to the food would be excluded by the 06 07 form. However, had the insured been covered by a 2002 or earlier edition of the Causes of Loss – Special Form (CP 10 30), the loss would be covered because these forms excluded only interruptions originating off-premises.

This change in the breadth of utility services protection increases the necessity of the **Utility Services – Direct Damage** endorsement (CP 04 17). If business income coverage is provided the **Utility Services – Time Element** (CP 15 45) endorsement is needed, too.

Utility Services – Direct Damage (CP 04 17)

Like the Causes of Loss – Special Form, **the Utility Services – Direct Damage** endorsement was among those updated in the 2007 revision. The endorsement was altered to dovetail with the revised exclusionary wording found in the Causes of Loss – Special Form. The new form language also removed the qualifying statement that the utility service property be located off premises. Coverage provided by this endorsement hinges on three main concepts: the utility services contemplated, the amount of coverage purchased, and the property covered by the endorsement.

Utility Services Contemplated

Losses arising out of the interruption of three main utility services divided into five classifications are eligible for coverage in this endorsement. Direct loss arising out of the interruption of water, power, and communications are eligible for protection.

Power and communications are further divided to include or exclude coverage for overhead power or communication lines. The insureds five options are:

- Water
- Power excluding overhead transmission lines
- Power including overhead transmission lines
- Communications excluding overhead transmission lines
- Communications including overhead transmission lines
- If coverage for overhead transmission lines is chosen, the premium is higher due to the increased exposure. However, if the insured location is served by overhead lines, this inclusion is necessary as these lines are more susceptible to covered damage than underground lines.

Amount of Coverage

Insureds may choose a specific limit of utility service damage protection. However, if a limit is specified, it is a sublimit of the total business personal property (BPP) limit specified in the underlying commercial property policy, not an additional limit of protection.

For example, the insured with a $500,000 business personal property limit and a $200,000 utility services sublimit has limited the amount of coverage available for a utility service loss to $200,000. These limits are not added together, making the utility service coverage amount a sublimit.

No amount has to be chosen. The limit can be left blank. If no amount is indicated, the insured has the full BPP limit (based on the classification of covered property) available to cover the loss. Further, the coinsurance condition does not apply to this limit, and there is no separate deductible. The advantage to the insured of using a lower limit for utility service losses is that the premium for this endorsement will be lower since it is not based on the full policy limit.

Covered Property

Within the endorsement, the insured can specify the type of property to which the utility service coverage is to attach. There is no apparent limitation on what can be written in as covered property. Examples of acceptable categories of covered property may include the following.

- All machinery and production equipment
- Perishable stock
- Business Personal Property
- All property

Before listing the property to be covered by the endorsement, a thorough analysis of the insured's property subject to damage by the interruption of a chosen utility is required. Additionally, the limit chosen must be adequate to cover the value of the property scheduled in this section of the policy.

Utility Services – Time Element (CP 15 45)

CP 15 45 was also updated in the 2007 property coverage revisions. It was altered to dovetail with the revised exclusionary wording found in the commercial property policy and Causes of Loss – Special Form. The new wording removed the qualifying statement requiring the utility service property be located outside a covered building.

In application, there is no coverage for the suspension of operations leading to a business income loss caused solely by an interruption of a supplied utility (water, communications, or power) in the unendorsed business income policy. CP 15 45 removes that exclusion, extending business income and extra expense protection should the supply from the chosen utility be interrupted. This endorsement, like the direct damage form, allows the insured the option of extending coverage to overhead transmission lines for both communication and power supply for an additional premium.

A separate limit of coverage must be chosen to cover the suspension caused by the disruption of the covered utility service(s). This loss does not fall under the policy's business income or extra expense limit, but neither does the coinsurance condition apply to the coverage provided by this endorsement.

Key Questions

- Does the insured's business depend on uninterrupted access to power, water or communication services?
- What could/would be the result of the interruption of any of these services?
- Do overhead transmission lines supply any of these services?
- Is there an on-premises generator?

- Are there any alternative means to supply the necessary services?

Chapter 11
Understanding Spoilage Coverage

Spoilage coverage is most commonly thought of in relation to restaurants and other like establishments, but the need for spoilage coverage goes far beyond food-based risks; in fact, there is a myriad of risk types that need the protection offered by the **Spoilage Coverage** (CP 04 40) endorsement.

To effectively recognize a spoilage exposure first requires knowledge of the breadth of coverage provided by the CP 04 40. These coverage provisions are discussed in this chapter.

Self-Contained Coverage – Sort Of

Although the **Spoilage Coverage** endorsement is attached to the commercial property policy, in some respects the CP 04 40 can be viewed as and treated as a self-contained policy. The endorsement specifically and narrowly defines covered property and goes on to limit the causes of loss available for that covered property to two named perils. Additionally, the endorsement is subject to its own limit and applies its own deductible.

Covered Property

Only perishable stock located at the premises described on the declarations is extended coverage by this endorsement; no other type of property is protected within its wording.

Perishable stock is defined to mean personal property *"Maintained under controlled conditions for its preservation; and Susceptible to loss or damage if the controlled conditions change."* A simple review of this definition of covered property opens up the broad realm of possible risk types in need of spoilage coverage.

Covered Causes of Loss

The CP 04 40 limits protection to two named causes of loss: Breakdown or Contamination; and Power Outage. One or both can be chosen when designing the coverage (it's better to combine the two). Each is defined by ISO as follows:

- ***Breakdown or contamination** means: 1) change in temperature or humidity resulting from mechanical breakdown or mechanical failure of refrigerating, cooling or humidity control apparatus or equipment, only while such equipment or apparatus is at the described premises and 2) contamination by the refrigerant.*

- ***Power outage** means change in temperature or humidity resulting from complete or partial interruption of electrical power, either on or off the described premises, due to conditions beyond your control.*

On the surface, the protection extended from these definitions appears very limited. However, the effective coverage is actually quite broad relative to the purpose of the endorsement. The endorsement protects the insured against the financial consequences of direct loss to listed personal property damaged or made unusable by: nearly any change in temperature, or contamination caused by a release of a refrigerant (which might be considered a pollutant otherwise).

Deductible

Simply, the deductible applicable to the underlying property coverage form is not applicable to the **Spoilage Coverage** endorsement. The insured can choose to use a deductible lower than, the same as, or higher than the deductible found in the underlying property coverage.

Comparison to Equipment Breakdown Coverage

Could an equipment breakdown policy be used in place of the **Spoilage Coverage** endorsement? This is a reasonable question. However, there are limitations in an equipment breakdown policy that make it an ineffective substitute for the CP 04 40.

Equipment breakdown (EB) forms define a covered loss as a breakdown to covered equipment. Initially this appears rather broad, but the definition of breakdown severely limits the coverage for perishable stock when compared to the spoilage coverage endorsement.

"Breakdown" within the EB forms is defined as: *"...direct physical loss that causes damage to 'Covered Equipment' and necessitates its repair or replacement."* The key phrase in this definition is, "and necessitates its repair or replacement." If the power just goes out or the equipment just wears out (this is not direct physical damage), any resulting spoilage loss is not covered. There must be some actual physical damage to equipment for the coverage to apply.

Protection provided by the spoilage coverage endorsement does not require that the equipment sustain physical damage necessitating repair. It only requires a failure or a power outage outside the insured's control.

Another possible issue with depending on an EB policy to provide spoilage coverage is that spoilage is not automatically provided in the form. To acquire spoilage coverage, there must be a limit chosen or the value of the raw material must be included in the limit of coverage and "Included" entered next to Spoilage on the EB's declaration page.

Equipment breakdown forms fill a lot of coverage gaps present in commercial property policies applying the special cause of loss form. However, EB should not be used as a substitute for the spoilage coverage as it is severely limited in its scope in relation to what triggers coverage. Insureds should consider using EB in conjunction with spoilage coverage to assure the broadest protection.

Two Major Spoilage Coverage Policy Provisions

Selling price and the presence of a refrigeration maintenance agreement are the two remaining major policy provisions found in the **Spoilage Coverage** form. Neither grants nor limits coverage. The selling price provision alters the valuation of the covered property following a loss; and the refrigeration maintenance agreement wording alters the rating and ultimate price of the coverage.

Selling Price

Property covered by the **Spoilage Coverage** endorsement is valued using the same valuation method applied to business personal property in the underlying commercial property policy. However, insureds have the option to alter the method of valuing covered property (perishable stock) following a covered loss by choosing the selling price option.

As its name suggests, this option changes the valuation method to the amount for which the insured was selling the product. Any applicable discounts and usual expenses (i.e., commissions) are subtracted from the selling price to arrive at the final value (to ensure that the payment does not violate the principle of indemnification).

If the selling price option is chosen, the insured must consider that value when choosing the limit of coverage. Although there is no coinsurance penalty, the insured should be fully protected.

Refrigeration Maintenance Agreement

Insureds can receive a 25 to 33 percent rate credit on the Breakdown/Contamination coverage, depending on the insured's classification, for having in place a refrigeration maintenance agreement. The rate credit does not apply to Power Outage coverage (if chosen).

A refrigeration maintenance agreement is simply a contract between the insured and a refrigeration service or maintenance company whereby the maintenance company agrees to inspect the subject equipment on a regular basis and perform necessary maintenance. The agreement must be maintained in full force for the entire policy period to prevent extreme consequences in relation to the coverage. The **Spoilage Coverage** form states: *"You must maintain a refrigeration maintenance or service agreement. If you voluntarily terminate this agreement and do not notify us, the insurance provided by this endorsement will be automatically suspended at the involved location."*

If the insurance carrier discovers the cancellation of a refrigeration maintenance agreement following an otherwise covered loss, they have the contractual right to deny coverage for failure to comply with policy provisions.

Policy Exclusions

Only five exclusions applicable to the underlying policy's property cause of loss form cross over to apply to the **Spoilage Coverage** endorsement. These are: earth movement, governmental action, nuclear hazard, war and military action, and water.

There are, however, five additional exclusions that apply specifically to this coverage endorsement. The policy reads:

"We will not pay for loss or damage caused by or resulting from:

a) *The disconnection of any refrigerating, cooling or humidity control system from the source of power.*

b) *The deactivation of electrical power caused by the manipulation of any switch or other device used to control the flow of electrical power or current.*

c) *The inability of an Electrical Utility Company or other power source to provide sufficient power due to:*

   1. *Lack of fuel, or*

   2. *Governmental order.*

d) *The inability of a power source at the described premises to provide sufficient power due to lack of generating capacity to meet demand.*

e) *Breaking of any glass that is a permanent part of any refrigerating, cooling, or humidity control unit."*

Examples of Spoilage Exposure Risks

One simple question can pinpoint those risks that have a spoilage exposure. "If you experience an extended loss of power, will any of your stock be destroyed, made unusable, or die?" The answer may reveal spoilage exposures where not previously considered. Common and uncommon examples of risks with a spoilage exposure include the following.

- Restaurants and all manner of food service risks
- Bakeries
- Ice cream stores (and mobile operations)
- Fruit and vegetable retailers
- Cheese stores
- Grocery stores, convenience stores, butchers, etc.
- Florists and greenhouses
- Pharmaceutical operations
- Food processing plants
- Cigar stores
- Tropical fish stores
- Blood banks (and like operations)
- Laboratories
- Cold storage warehouses

Obviously, this is not an all-inclusive list of risks with a spoilage exposure, but this may prove that there are a lot of insureds with a spoilage exposure requiring this coverage.

Key Questions

- If the insured experiences an extended power outage, will any stock be destroyed, made unusable, or die?
- How long would the outage have to last for the stock to be destroyed?
- Describe the perishable property.
- What is the value of this property?

Chapter 12

Understanding Leasehold
Interest Protection

The **Leasehold Interest Coverage Form** (CP 00 60)
protects the insured tenant from the potential of an additional
financial catastrophe due to the loss of a favorable lease arising
out of the inability to occupy the leased space following a
covered cause of loss. A lease is considered favorable when the
rate per square foot, or however the rent is calculated, is
somewhat or substantially less than comparable space
available in the local commercial real estate market. In broader
terms, the tenant is paying less than market rates for the space.

There are many reasons for the existence of a favorable
lease. A market bust may cause property owners to offer
favorable leases to attract or retain tenants. Sometimes
insureds have occupied space as a tenant for so many years
that the periodic increases have not kept up with the local real
estate market. Or there may be situations where the property
owner wanted to keep a strong relationship with the tenant.

Regardless of the reason, the tenant has a lease rate that
cannot be replicated in the subject real estate market should
the need to find a comparable location arise. Losing a favorable
lease following a specified event can result in an unplanned

increase in operational expenses for years following the actual damage and the business's return to operational normalcy.

Consider the insured whose lease is cancelled in the first year of a 5-year agreement because the building suffers major property damage (major is a subjective term, but in this context it signifies enough damage to allow the landlord to cancel the lease). The insured is forced to either find a new location from which to operate or accept a renegotiated lease at a higher cost.

Suppose market prices in the example area are $15 per square foot rather than the $10 per square foot the insured is paying under the current lease. To lease an equivalent 20,000 square feet, as previously occupied, the monthly lease jumps from $16,667 to $25,000. The difference in monthly rent translates into $100,000 in additional annual operating costs due solely to increased lease payments. Even an insured occupying only 2,000 square feet, applying the information surrounding this sample market, would experience an increase in annual lease expenses of $10,000. (This example is referenced throughout this chapter.)

Leasehold Interest Coverage

Like business income, leasehold interest coverage protects against the financial consequences of an indirect loss arising out of a direct loss. Three conditions apply to leasehold interest protection: 1) there must be direct property damage 2) resulting from a covered cause of loss 3) directly leading to the cancellation of a favorable lease. The policy responds only if all three requirements are met.

Note that leasehold interest coverage does not pay the cost to rent an alternate location while the building is being repaired; that's the job of extra expense coverage (included with or separate from business income protection).

Tenants lease interest, bonus payments, tenant's improvements and betterments, and prepaid rent are the four exposures insured by leasehold interest coverage. Insureds may or may not be subject to all four expense classes.

Tenants Lease Interest (TLI)

TLI is primary leasehold interest exposure. Tenants lease interest is the difference between the rent/lease actually paid by the tenant and the market value of the premises. In the previous example, the monthly TLI (or gross leasehold interest) is $8,333 ($100,000 per year). If, at the time of the loss, the insured has 30 months remaining on its lease, the insured's total TLI is $249,990. Total TLI is not the amount of coverage purchased; only the net TLI is insured. The net TLI is a function of the time value of money (discussed in a later section).

Bonus Payments

Tenants may offer to or landlords may suggest the purchase of a favorable lease. A bonus payment is nonrefundable money paid by the tenant to acquire the reduced lease (this is not equivalent to a security deposit). For instance, the property owner in the example, though aware of the premise's current market value, agrees to lease the space to the tenant at $10 per square foot rather than the market value $15 per square foot for an upfront payment of $100,000. The property owner gains an immediate infusion of revenue and a long-term tenant in a previously unoccupied (thus unprofitable) space; and the tenant gains a favorable lease that saves it $200,000 over the term of the lease (not accounting for the time value of money and the required internal rate of return).

Tenant's Improvements and Betterments

Improvements and betterments are additions and upgrades made to the real property by the tenant. Once made part of the building (real property), they cannot be removed and thus become the property of the building owner. This coverage part protects the tenant for its loss of use interest in the property, again, if the favorable lease is cancelled and the insured does not return to the property following a covered direct loss. However, the **Leasehold Interest Coverage** form does not respond if the improvements and betterments are separately and specifically insured on the property policy (as that would constitute multiple payments for the same property).

Prepaid Rent

As the name suggests, this is rent the tenant pays in advance that is not returned, even if the lease is cancelled. Following the direct property loss and the resulting loss of the favorable lease terms insured by the leasehold interest policy, the amount of the insured's loss is calculated based on the number of months left in the lease at the time of the loss.

How to Calculate the Leasehold Interest Exposure

Two values must be developed before calculating the amount of leasehold interest coverage purchased: gross leasehold interest (GLI) and monthly leasehold interest (MLI).

Gross Leasehold Interest (GLI)

Gross Leasehold interest (GLI) is the difference between the monthly rental market value of the property and what the tenant is actually paying each month. Notice that gross leasehold interest is calculated on a monthly basis. The monthly GLI is multiplied by an interest rate factor based on the number of months left in the lease to develop the amount of coverage to purchase (detailed in the next section). This is the basis for the insured tenants' lease interest (TLI) coverage. In the referenced example, the GLI was $8,333.

The GLI may require recalculation at every renewal, with no more than 2 years between reviews. The reason: the market value of a property fluctuates over time. When coverage is first written there may be a $3-per-square-foot difference between market value and the amount actually paid. Two years into the lease, the commercial real estate market may have boomed resulting in a $5-per-square-foot difference between the lease payments and the market value. The reverse is also true.

Calculating the GLI is rather simple; the difficulty arises in determining the market rental value of the subject premises. Market rental value may be garnered from the tenant who is well aware of his favorable lease and knows the premises' true rental value; but more likely the information is available from local property rental value reports published by area commercial realtors. (Large commercial real estate brokerage firms often publish rental reports listing average per-square-foot costs based on the occupancy type (e.g., office, industrial, manufacturing, retail, etc.) and the location.) Regardless of the source, this information will necessitate research.

Monthly Leasehold Interest (MLI)

Monthly leasehold interest (MLI) accounts for the three remaining leasehold interest coverage exposures: bonus payments,
improvements and betterments, and prepaid rents. Plus, developing MLI is simpler than calculating gross leasehold interest (GLI) as only three pieces of information are required: a) the amount of the expenditure, b) when the expenditure was made, and c) how many months were left in the lease when the expenditure was made. The formula used to calculate the MLI based on this information is:

Original Cost / Number of Months Left in the Lease at time of expenditure = MLI

Assume, for example, the tenant paid the property owner $100,000 as a bonus payment to obtain a favorable 36-month lease at $10 per square foot rather than the market rental value of $15 per square foot. All the information is there to calculate

145

the MLI for the bonus payment. Since the expenditure was made at the beginning of the lease, the bonus payment MLI is $2,777.78 ($100,000/36 months).

The same three pieces of data and calculation methods are used to develop the MLI for all three expenditure classifications listed above. However, since the expenditures may occur at different times, the total costs cannot simply be added together because the amount of time remaining for the tenant to enjoy the use interest of the investments differs based on when the expenditure is made within the lease period. Each MLI must be calculated separately. Essentially there are three MLIs.

Staying with the example tenant above: one year into the lease the tenant makes $200,000 in structural building modifications to fit its operational needs. Since these are real property changes, the tenant has only a use interest in the property as they cannot remove them. The tenant's improvements and betterments MLI is $8,333.33 ($200,000/24 months). Remember, improvements and betterments coverage in the leasehold interest form only applies if there is no other coverage on this property.

How GLI and MLI Apply

Neither the gross leasehold interest (GLI) amount nor the monthly leasehold interest (MLI) amount is used as the coverage amount when purchasing leasehold interest coverage. Both must be converted to their individual net amounts to develop the amount of coverage purchased, the net leasehold interest (NLI).

Developing the amount of Coverage Purchased – The Net

NLI is the amount of coverage actually purchased. The **Leasehold Interest Coverage** form assigns two definitions to this term depending on the exposure being considered. Tenants' lease interest's definition of NLI applies the time value of money to the gross leasehold interest (GLI) to develop the final coverage amount. The three remaining exposures base the definition of NLI on the monthly leasehold interest (MLI) and the amount of time left in the lease when the policy is written. Both calculations are explained below.

Net Leasehold Interest (NLI) and Tenants' Lease Interest (TLI)

Tenants' lease interest (TLI) is the primary leasehold interest exposure. The loss of a favorable lease, as demonstrated earlier in the chapter, can increase the insured's operational expenses long after the actual loss and return to operation.

TLI's NLI calculation is based loosely on the time value of money, specifically a hybrid present value of a dollar calculation. The two beginning factors in NLI's calculation are the previously-calculated gross leasehold interest (GLI) (the monthly difference between market value and the actual lease payment) and the number of months left in the subject lease at the inception date of the policy (if the agent is working many days in advance, it is important to remember the calculation begins with the policy's inception date).

Unfortunately, that is the only easy part of the NLI calculation. The next choice made is the expected rate of return the insured would earn if, rather than paying rent, they invested the money. ISO has filed 11 present value factor forms ranging from a 5 percent to a 15 percent rate of return. Once the insured estimates the amount of interest that could be earned investing rather than paying rent, the calculation can resume.

Again, using the example presented earlier:

- The developed GLI: $8,333
- Number of months left in the lease at policy inception: 30
- The chosen interest rate (rate of return): 5%

Applying the above information and using the "Leasehold Interest Factors for 5%" (CP 60 05), the TLI is $234,867.30 ($8,333 x 28.1852). Without the application of the hybrid present value calculation, the insured value would be $249,990. But because the insured has yet to suffer the lease expense, the total difference in TLI is not used in the limit's calculation.

At renewal, the insured TLI value must be recalculated. Twelve months have passed, so the tenant has only 18 months remaining in the lease at policy inception. The new TLI net leasehold interest is $144,342.60 ($8,333 x 17.3218).

Two questions arise in the above example. What if the lease renews in the middle of the policy period? And what if the economy will not allow any small company to make 5 percent on their money: is there any option to use a lower percentage and interpolate the factors?

If the lease renews midterm, the coverage will have to be rewritten midterm to account for the lease's new terms and conditions, the likely altered gross leasehold interest and the new lease period. Second, the rules, according to ISO, do not contemplate percentages different than those provided by the filed endorsements.

As stated earlier, these factors are hybrid simple-interest present value calculations. The reason the term hybrid is applied is based on how they appear to be developed. Since these factors are monthly rather than annual periods, the interest rate is divided by 12 and thus becomes a monthly interest rate; however, the developed monthly interest rate does not match the amount a simple interest, present value calculation produces over several months.

Net Leasehold Interest (NLI) and Monthly Leasehold Interest (MLI)

Once each of the three MLIs are individually calculated as previously detailed, they are added together to generate the total monthly leasehold interest (TMLI). To develop the value of the second definition of NLI, the TMLI is multiplied by the number of months left in the lease at the inception date of the policy.

149

Referring once again to the previously presented sample tenant, and rounding to the nearest dollar, their total MLI is $11,111 calculated as follows:

- Bonus Payment MLI: $2,777.78
- Tenant's I&B: $8,333.33
- Prepaid Rent: $0

With 18 months remaining in the lease at the inception date of the policy, the MLI net leasehold interest is $199,998 ($11,111 x 18 months).

Combining the two definitions of net leasehold interest, the total amount of coverage this insured should purchase with 18 months remaining in the lease is $344,340.60 ($144,342.60 + $199,998). This is definitely an exposure worth insuring.

Loss Calculation

Although the amount of coverage listed on the **Leasehold Interest Coverage Schedule** (CP DS 07) is based on both definitions of NLI, the amount of loss payment is based on the number of months left in the lease at the time of the loss. The policy specifically states that the coverage amount decreases as each month passes.

Calculating Net Leasehold Interest Loss for Tenants' Lease Interest (TLI)

At the inception date of the previously used example policy, there were 18 months left in the lease. Multiplying the gross leasehold interest (GLI) by the 5 percent leasehold interest factor found in the applicable endorsement (CP 60 05) produced a TLI net leasehold interest of $144,342.60.

Assume that 6 months into the policy period, the building suffered major damage causing the insured tenant to lose its favorable lease. Only 12 months remain on the cancelled lease at the time of the loss.

Because the insured tenant benefited from the favorable lease for the first 6 months of the policy, paying a leasehold interest loss for that period would violate the principle of indemnification. To uphold indemnification, the TLI net leasehold interest is recalculated at the time of the loss. The new (and recoverable) TLI net leasehold interest is calculated by multiplying the previously developed GLI ($8,333) by the 12-month interest rate factor found in the endorsement used at inception—5 percent in this example.

Applying the relevant information and forms to this example, the recoverable TLI is $97,397.77 ($8,333 x 11.6882). However, this is the maximum the insured can receive. If the landlord cancels the lease due to the direct property loss but renegotiates the lease with the tenant, still at lower than market rates, the insured will get the lesser of the recoverable TLI or the difference between the old lease and new lease for the *remainder* of the prior lease's term. Recall that market value in our example is $15 per square foot; the tenant pays only $10 per square foot. In the aftermath of the direct property loss, the property owner cancels the lease, but renegotiates a new one with the tenant at $12.50 per square foot. The tenant does suffer increased operational cost, but not to the amount anticipated.

At $10 per square foot, the tenant's monthly lease payment was $16,666.67. Under the renegotiated lease ($12.50 per square foot), the tenant's monthly payment is $20,833.33—a monthly difference of $4,166.66. Because there were 12 months left in the lease at the time of the loss, the insured tenant receives $49,999.92 (really should be rounded up to $50,000) for his TLI loss (the lesser of the two calculations, as per the policy form).

Calculating Net Leasehold Interest Loss for All Other Leasehold Interest Exposures

Essentially, the same provisions applicable to a TLI loss settlement apply to the remaining three leasehold interest exposures. The amount of coverage is reduced monthly during the policy period, and the amount of coverage calculated at the date of loss is the maximum the insured tenant receives.

In the loss presented above, the insured has enjoyed use of the premises for 6 months, thus the amount subject to loss, and payable, is reduced from $199,998 to $133,332 ($11,111 x 12 months remaining in the lease). But again, this is the maximum the insured can receive. Should the landlord agree to allow the tenant to continue using the premises by renegotiating the lease or through some other arrangement, the leasehold interest policy states that the insured shall receive the lesser of the loss sustained or the net leasehold interest at the time of the loss.

Calculating the loss sustained may be complicated by the presence of insurance on the improvements and betterments or the landlord's crediting of the bonus payment towards the new $12.50-per-square-foot lease (rather than the $15-per-square-foot market value). Providing a simplified actual loss sustained example for these expenditures is difficult. Agents just need to be aware of this provision.

One key point concerning both of these loss calculations is that the policy pays for the entire time remaining in the lease, not the policy. If there are 30 months left in the lease, yet only 6 months remaining in the policy period, this coverage pays for the 30-month loss.

Vacancy Provisions

Simply, if the tenant insured under this coverage form vacates the building for more than 60 consecutive days, and the building meets the definition of vacant, there is no coverage if a lease-cancelling property loss occurs.

Vacancy as applied within the policy form includes two conditions: vacant and unoccupied. "Vacant" means there is nothing in the building. "Unoccupied" generally connotes that there is not enough equipment or furniture to conduct normal operations. (Placing a desk and chair in a building insured as a manufacturing operation does not negate the fact that it is unoccupied and thus vacant.) If either condition exists, the vacancy provision applies.

However, the existence of a sublease alters the vacancy provision (and exclusion). With a sublease in place, the

vacancy provision in the leasehold form mimics the same
provision in the Commercial Property form stating:

1. *We will not pay for any loss or damage caused by
   any of the following even if they are Covered
   Causes of Loss:*

   a) Vandalism;

   *b) Sprinkler leakage, unless you have protected
   the system against freezing;*

   c) Building glass breakage;

   d) Water damage;

   e) Theft; or

   f) Attempted theft.

2. *With respect to a Covered Cause of Loss not listed
   in (1) (a) through (1)(f) above, we will reduce the
   amount we would otherwise pay for the loss or
   damage by 15%.*

Conclusion

There is no better way for an agent to set himself or herself
apart than to note and present exposures the insured has never
considered or been apprised of. Leasehold interest coverage is
likely one of these exposures. First, agents must understand
the coverage, and then they must be able to explain the
coverage to the insured.

As seen in the examples provided in this chapter, the
amount of exposure can be rather high; certainly the insured
should be willing to protect such investments. Market

conditions along with other factors influence the need for this coverage.

Key Questions

- Does the lease agreement allow the landlord to cancel the lease? Under what conditions?

- How does the cost of the insured's lease compare with the local real estate market?

- Could comparable space be leased at or near the same price?

- What is the market cost per square foot in the area? Where was this information found?

- What would comparable space cost?

- Did the tenant/insured make any upgrades to the real property that would remain with the building owner? What was the cost? When were the updates made?

- Did the tenant make any payments to secure a lower lease payment?

- Has the insured made any prepaid rent payments that cannot be recovered if the lease is cancelled?

- How many months left in the lease at the beginning of the policy term? How many left at the end of the policy term? Will the lease renew during the policy term?

Chapter 13

Three Commercial Property Endorsements Every Client Should Have

Three key Commercial Property Policy (CPP) endorsements every insured should consider are the: **Additional Covered Property** endorsement (CP 14 10 or state-specific form), **Additional Building Property** endorsement (CP 14 15), and **Joint or Disputed Loss Agreement** (CP 12 70). Obviously these are not the only commercial property endorsements valuable to a specific insured, but these are three every insured should consider when building coverage.

Additional Covered Property Endorsement (CP 14 10)

Within the CPP is a long list of property not covered. Scattered throughout this list of excluded property are several types of real or personal property the insured (and possibly even the agent) may assume is covered by the policy when, in fact, they are not. Examples include building foundations, underground pipes, flues or drains, and fencing.

Some excluded property can be added back to the list of covered property and removed from the list of property not covered via the **Additional Covered Property** endorsement. Two broad versions of the form are available from ISO, depending on the state in question.

- **The CP 14 10.** This is essentially a blank form allowing the insured to specifically list the property they wish to remove from the property not covered list and include as covered property.

- **ISO State-specific endorsements.** Two examples are North Carolina's CP 14 11 and Virginia's CP 14 12. In forms such as these, several types of real and personal property are taken from the list of property not covered within the unendorsed coverage form and listed on the endorsement. The insured chooses which property it desires to include as covered property and indicates that choice by placing an "X" in the box next to that property class.

Any removal of property from the property not covered list and its endorsed inclusion on the covered property list is, of course, subject to underwriter approval regardless of which version of the form is used.

Interestingly, some of the real property found on the property not covered list is often included when the building's replacement cost is calculated yet excluded at the time of loss. Foundations and the cost of excavations, grading, filling, and backfilling are good examples. These values and costs are excluded, but the building cannot be rebuilt unless and until this prep work is completed.

A building's foundation can be severely damaged by certain causes of loss (especially fire); tearing up, removing, and replacing the damaged foundation can be expensive. The unendorsed commercial property policy excludes coverage for these costs. Further, before the replacement foundation can be laid, the land must be graded, possibly even requiring some excavation. These costs, too, are excluded in the unendorsed CPP. Using the **Additional Covered Property** endorsement to add just these two otherwise excluded expenses make the endorsement a near must-have for insureds responsible for insuring the building. Just remember to include these values/costs in the building value.

Other key real property normally excluded from coverage which can be added back under these endorsements include: exterior fencing, retaining walls, underground pipes, flues or drains, underground tanks, bulkheads, pilings, piers, wharves, docks, bridges, roadways, walks, patios, and other paved surfaces. Some personal property also can be moved to the covered property list by use of the **Additional Covered Property** endorsement including: vehicles or self-propelled machines (including watercraft and aircraft) and animals.

Nearly every insured in need of real property coverage should consider this endorsement to extend the definition of covered property. Building owners and tenants required to provide building coverage can greatly benefit from this endorsement. Agents should use the list of property not covered as a tool to help them manage the client's insurance risk. Combined, the exclusionary list and the endorsement can be used like a checklist to confirm that all the insured's exposures have been discovered and discussed.

Additional Building Property

Is a particular piece of insured property considered building or business personal property? Unless the intent is made clear up front, the answer might be subject to interpretation following a loss. The unique purpose of the **Additional Building Property** (CP 14 15) endorsement is to specifically cover property that can be considered either real or personal property as building to avoid gray areas at the time of loss.

"Permanently installed machinery and equipment" is defined as part of the building within the CPP. "Machinery and equipment" is also listed under the definition of business personal property. The difference is obviously the term "permanently installed." However, what constitutes permanent installation? Does it mean bolted to the floor or wall such that removal would cause damage to the building proper? What about equipment that is bolted to real property (making it real property by definition), but which can be removed easily leaving no signs of damage after some minor repair? A few examples of permanently installed equipment might include a pipe organ in a church; semi-permanently installed equipment, chairs and tables bolted to the floor in dental and medical offices; and production machinery simply bolted to a concrete floor to keep it from vibrating out of place. Although not an all-inclusive list, this provides an example of the gray area of permanently installed.

Another potentially fuzzy loss is loss to real property improvements and betterments made by the tenant in a leased space. The definition of business personal property extends to include the tenant's use interest in their improvements and betterments; but what about the value of the improvements and betterments if, as is likely the case, the tenant has to pay to replace the improvements and betterments following a loss?

Completed additions are included within the CPP's definition of building. This term theoretically encompasses improvements and betterments but not explicitly. It is preferable to specifically endorse the policy to include tenant's improvement and betterments as part of the building than depend on an interpretation after the loss.

Anytime property can be covered as building rather than business personal property, the insured should take the opportunity. The reason: the rate is lower for building than for business personal property. Another reason to consider this endorsement is coverage limits. If the insured considers and includes some property under the building limits, yet the insurance carrier considers it business personal property when adjusting the loss, there may be a coinsurance penalty.

Of course this problem can be fixed by using blanket limits. But remember, the use of blanket limits requires the attachment of the **Statement of Values** (CP 16 15) endorsement and coverage limits equal to 90 percent of the insured value.

To activate coverage in the **Additional Building Property** (CP 14 15) endorsement, the insured lists the building number, the premises number, and describes the property to be defined as building. The endorsement states that the property listed in the schedule is considered part of the building coverage and is no longer considered business personal property.

Most insureds have property that could be considered either real or personal property; use this endorsement to remove any question or debate that may arise following a loss.

Joint or Disputed Loss Agreement

Use and discussion of this endorsement is based on the presupposition that the insured has in place Equipment Breakdown coverage (formerly known as Boiler and Machinery). Every insured has an Equipment Breakdown exposure and should buy the protection.

A detailed discussion of Equipment Breakdown coverage is outside the intended scope of this chapter; however, it must be noted that Equipment Breakdown protection fills several causes of loss gaps present in the Commercial Property Policy (CPP). Examples include loss to equipment (such as HVAC and telephone equipment) caused by power surge, explosion of steam pipes, boilers, etc. and other such loss or damage.

When there is a CPP and a separate Equipment Breakdown Policy in place there is the possibility that one loss can encompass and trigger both coverage forms. With two carriers involved, there is the possibility that any loss payment will be delayed as the carriers attempt to piece together the incident and decide which carrier should pay the bulk of the claim. This is where the **Joint or Disputed Loss Agreement** endorsement comes into play.

The **Joint or Disputed Loss Agreement** (CP 12 70) endorsement simply requires the CPP and equipment breakdown carrier to pay the insured for the disputed loss as soon as the policy provisions are met (filing of a proof of loss, agreement on the insurable amount of damage, etc.) without holding the insured hostage while the carriers debate the amount of each carrier's liability for the loss. The form requires both carriers to pay half of the disagreed upon loss and then arbitrate between themselves after the insured has been indemnified.

Once the insured has been made whole, the insurance carriers continue their arbitration until two out of three arbitrators agree on the split of liability. The insurer found the most liable must reimburse the other carrier the difference between the 50 percent already paid and their actual liability, plus liquidated damages. Liquidated damages are developed by multiplying the highest prime rate in effect on the day the agreement is invoked by 1.5. That percentage rate is applied during the period of arbitration (period of Liquidated Damages).

For the insured to benefit from the provisions of the **Joint or Disputed Loss Agreement**, both the CPP and the Equipment Breakdown Policy must contain this provision, either by endorsement or by inclusion in the form. Commercial property policies must generally be endorsed, while many equipment breakdown forms include the wording in the policy language. Regardless, both forms must contain this provision.

A simple way to avoid the problem is to use a combined commercial property/ equipment breakdown policy.

Conclusion

The two most important property coverages every commercial insured should purchase are business income and ordinance or law protection. Beyond those, the three detailed commercial property endorsements discussed in this chapter should also be considered for and by every commercial property insured.

Chapter 14

Understanding the Unique
Facets of Flood Insurance

"I don't need flood insurance; I'm not in a 'flood zone.'" Or, "I don't need flood insurance because my mortgage company said I don't need it." These statements are made more often than any insurance professional would like to admit. But the frightening part is many agents might agree with the statements without questioning or understanding the full fallacy of either statement.

Every structure located in one of the more than 20,400 NFIP- participating communities is in a "flood zone." The insured's house or building may simply not be in one of the more hazardous zones. In this situation, the client is really trying to say, "I don't need flood insurance because I'm not in a Special Flood Hazard Area (SFHA)." The reality is that the client just doesn't know the correct terminology, but agents must know and be able to effectively and tactfully correct the client/insured when discussing flood coverage. And, as will be seen, being located outside a SFHA does not guarantee freedom from the possibility of flood loss.

Other often used misnomers in news reports and newspapers are "100-year flood plain," or the "100-year flood event." Although the creation and use of both terms makes some sense based on the statistical calculations used to establish hazardous flood areas— both give the wrong impression of the true hazard. Furthermore, "flood zone," "100-year flood plain," and "100-year flood event" are three phrases favored by the media and perpetuated by clients (and some agents). These over-simplified attempts to describe Special Flood Hazard Areas (SFHAs) are incorrectly applied to the true exposure faced.

Defining Special Flood Hazard Areas (SFHAs)

A Special Flood Hazard Area (SFHA) is defined as an area having a 1 percent chance of being inundated by flood waters in any given year (thus the creation and misuse of the term "100-year flood plain"). Flood waters have an equal chance of submerging these areas every year for 5 straight years, or not at all for 200 years; there is simply a 1 percent statistical possibility every year. Homes located in SFHAs have a 26 percent chance of suffering flood damage during a normal 30-year loan according to FEMA.

There are two broad classifications of SFHAs: "A" zones and "V" zones. Further information about these zones can often be found on Flood Insurance Rate Maps (FIRMs), further outlined by use of subclassifications such as "AR," "AO," or "VO." These and other SFHA subclassifications provide more detailed information about the pattern and characteristics of flooding in the specified area. Detailed information about each of the Special Flood Hazard Area subclassifications can be found on FEMA's website.

What Makes a "V" a "V"?

Differentiating between "A" zones and "V" zones is relatively simple: "V" zones are generally located near areas subject to hazardous tidal flows (waves) such as the ocean. "A" zones are those areas simply subject to inundation by overflow of rivers, low-lying areas subject to ponding, etc. "V" can be used to signify "velocity"; the water is flowing with the increased hazard and damage of wave action. "A" can mean "altitude"; the water goes up and goes back down, but it lacks the damaging wave action of a "V" zone.

When reviewing a coastal Flood Insurance Rate Map (FIRM), it is common to find "V" zones morph into "A" zones. Both areas are still Special Flood Hazard Areas, but there's a difference in the supposed hazard and potential damage leading to different rating criteria. A common question is, "How is that point decided? Where does a "V" become an "A"?"

To establish this point, engineers must calculate two heights: the "100-year" still-water height and wave heights above the still-water height. Wave height decreases the further up the shore it moves; when the anticipated height of the tidal wave falls to less than 3 feet above the "100-year" still-water height, the "V" zone ends and the "A" zone begins. "Base Flood Elevation" (BFE) and "100-year" still-water height are not synonymous. The BFE includes some wave action in its calculation.

Agents who write flood coverage do not necessarily need this information for rating purposes, but it is essential to understand it when discussing coverage and rating with a client. Removing some of the mystery in flood insurance can put the client more at ease.

"A" and "V" Zone Differences

Reference points used for rating policies in Special Flood Hazard Areas differ depending on a structure's zonal location. "A" zones use the bottom of the first elevated floor as the reference point for calculating the height above (or below) Base Flood Elevation. Conversely, "V" zones use the bottom of the lowest horizontal support for the measuring point. "V" zone reference points could be as much as 18 inches to 2 feet lower than "A" zone reference points. Why is the bottom of the lowest horizontal support used in a "V" zone? Due to the damage potential presented by wave action.

"A" and "V" zones also differ regarding the acceptable means for elevating the insured structure. Structures located in "A" zones may be elevated above Base Flood Elevation (BFE) either by pilings, columns, shear walls, or a solid foundation perimeter wall with appropriate openings. Conversely, pilings, columns, shear walls, or "breakaway" walls are the only acceptable elevation methods in "V" zones.

Proper openings in a solid foundation perimeter wall (eligible only in "A" zones) allow for the free passage of water into and out of the building without requiring human intervention to open or close. Other NFIP requirements for these openings are: a minimum of two openings on different sides of each enclosed area, at least 1 square inch of opening for each square foot of enclosed space, the bottom of the openings can be no more than 1 foot above the grade immediately below the vent and windows, doors, and garage doors are not considered proper openings (they require human intervention). If the "A" zone structure lacks sufficient openings as defined, the reference point becomes the ground under the structure.

Pilings, columns, shear walls, or "breakaway" walls are the only NFIP allowable method for elevating a structure in "V" zones. Following is a description of two of these options.

- **Shear Wall** – A shear wall is a structural support running parallel (as nearly as possible) to the flow of the water. These walls are not structurally joined at the ends allowing for water to flow through unimpeded.

- **Breakaway Walls** – Breakaway walls are non-structural walls perpendicular to the flow of water (taking the direct hit) designed to fail under certain wave force conditions. The failure of these walls should cause no damage to the structural supports, the foundation, or any part of the building above the walls.

Supposed "Non-hazardous" Flood Zones

Non-special flood hazard areas, historically delineated using "B," "C," or "X," are considered areas of moderate or minimal hazard generally only expected to flood in times of severe storms or when drainage problems exist. However, FEMA states that 25 percent to 30 percent of all flood insurance claims are paid in these "less hazardous" areas; so neither insureds nor agents should ignore flood insurance just because they are not in areas considered hazardous.

Zones historically labeled "B" and "C" are being replaced with just "X." As Flood Insurance Rate Maps (FIRMs) are updated, non-SFHAs will be assigned a "Shaded X" or simply an (unshaded) "X." Base Flood Elevations are not indicated in either "X" zone.

"Shaded X" zones correspond to areas with a higher probability of flooding than areas tagged by an unshaded "X." A "Shaded X" indicates the area has a 0.2 percent annual chance of flooding (the "500-year" flood line) or a 1 percent chance of experiencing flooding of less than one foot in any given year (not high enough to be classified as a Special Flood Hazard Area).

Agents with clients depending on Difference in Condition (DIC) policies to provide flood coverage must pay close attention to the flood coverage exclusions in the DIC policy. Some DIC forms exclude flood outright or increase the flood deductible to match the maximum available coverage offered by NFIP policies for structures located in Special Flood Hazard Areas ("A" and "V" zones) and Shaded "X" zones. This "Shaded X" wording is often thrown in without the agent's or insured's knowledge. If such limitation cannot be negotiated out, then the insured must be informed, and any structures located in "Shaded X" zones must be covered by an NFIP policy.

Areas where the flood hazard is undetermined are shown on the FIRMs as a zone "D." This zone may also be used when one community incorporates portions of another community where no map has been previously prepared.

Zone Lines: More than One Zone

Flood zones do not follow property boundary lines; they are a function of the water source, protective measures, erosion, drainage, and other hydrological factors. Zones may change in the middle of an individual's yard or in the middle of the living room. Questions often arise as to when the more hazardous zone must be used?

The more hazardous zone is used with any part of the structure or its permanent, real-property attachments is dissected by the zone line, even if it is a part of the structure not covered by the flood policy. If the deck attached at the rear of the house is partially in an "A" zone and partially in an "X" zone, the entire house is rated in the "A" zone, even though the deck is not covered by the flood policy.

Further, if the line is in the back yard, rating is based on the zone in which the house is located. It is not the zone of the land that matters; it is the zones in which the structure itself is located.

Flood Policy Forms

Compared to more common property insurance policies, National Flood Insurance Program (NFIP) policy forms are actually quite intriguing. First, the Federal government wrote them; and second, they use terms and conditions not found in other property policy forms. The three most commonly used NFIP coverage forms are highlighted below.

Three Policy Forms

Each Standard Flood Insurance Policy (SFIP) form issued by the Federal Emergency Management Agency (FEMA) specifies the terms, conditions, and agreement between FEMA (as the insurer) and the named insured. Provisions are essentially the same among the three forms with the only differences being the qualifications for coverage, the limits available and the property valuation methods applied.

Dwelling Form

Approximately 85 percent of current NFIP policies are written using the dwelling form. It is designed for one- to four-family structures primarily occupied as a residence. Homeowners, residential renters, owners of two- to four-unit residential structures, residential townhouse or row house owners, and the owner of an individual unit in a condominium building are eligible for the dwelling form.

Property insured on the dwelling form is valued at replacement cost provided two requirements are met:

- Property is insured to at least 80 percent of its value or the maximum coverage available—whichever is less; and

- The insured lives in the residence at least 80 percent of the year.

If either of these requirements is not met, the most the insured is going to receive is the property's actual cash value (ACV).

Although the policy states that replacement cost is paid if 80 percent of the value is carried, this is not a coinsurance form. Like the homeowners' form, the dwelling form will pay the greater of actual cash value or the amount developed in the coinsurance calculation; but only if the insured lives there 80 percent of the year. If both conditions are not met, losses are paid at actual cash value. This is the reason this is not the equivalent of a coinsurance form.

In regular program communities, coverage for buildings and contents are limited to a specified maximum. Current (as of 2018) maximum limits are $250,000 on the structure and $100,000 on contents (which applies to renters as well).

General Property Form

Owners or lessees of "other residential" and nonresidential structures or units are eligible for protection under the general property form. Residential structures with five or more units, hotel or motels, apartment buildings, cooperative condominiums, assisted living facilities and dormitories are examples of "other residential" structures insurable on the general property form. Nonresidential structures, as is evidenced by the name, are any structures where people do not live and includes stores, office buildings, manufacturing facilities, warehouses, churches, schools, detached garages, commercial condominiums, and any other eligible structure not normally considered a place of residence.

Structures and contents insured on the general property form are valued at actual cash value with no other options available.

Maximum limits differ depending on the classification of the structure. "Other residential" structures are limited to $500,000 on the structure and $100,000 on the contents. Nonresidential structures are eligible for up to $500,000 on the building and another $500,000 for the contents.

Residential Condominium Building Association Policy (RCBAP)

The Residential Condominium Building Association Policy provides building coverage and, if desired, can be used to provide contents coverage for common use personal property for residential condominium buildings, provided 75 percent or more of the building is residential use. Coverage is written in the name of the association for the benefit of the association and the unit owners. Only buildings with a condominium form of ownership are eligible for this coverage form. The unit owners must take title and deed to specific units.

Cooperative condominiums are not eligible for the RCBAP as title to a specific unit is not passed to the occupier of the unit; an "owner" buys stock in the cooperative and is allowed to live in a particular unit (based on the amount of stock purchased). Timeshare buildings *may* be eligible for the RCBAP if condominium-style ownership is offered in jurisdictions which allow that title to individual units be vested in the owners' names (a fee simple-type arrangement allowing the title to be transferred to heirs).

Property insured on the RCBAP is valued at replacement cost. In fact, this is the only form that offers a true coinsurance clause similar to the homeowners' or commercial property policy.

Much higher limits are available for buildings insurable under the RCBAP. Up to $250,000 per unit, per building is available. For example, an insured can purchase up to $2.5 million in protection for a 10-unit building. Coverage for commonly owned personal property is limited to $100,000 per building.

Participating Communities in the Regular Program

Two requirements must be met before owners or lessees can avail themselves of the coverage and limits highlighted above:

- The structure must be in a participating community (currently over 21,800).
- The community must have transitioned into the Regular Program.

A participating community is one that has been notified by FEMA through the Federal Insurance and Mitigation Administration (FIMA) that there are flood-prone areas within the community (usually resulting from previous floods), has been notified of the location of those areas by publication of a Flood Hazard Boundary Map, within 1 year of notification agrees to join NFIP and agrees to participate in the development of local flood plain management guidelines.

Being labeled a participating community is the first step toward becoming a regular community.

Immediately following a community's decision to participate with NFIP, the emergency program is made available to residents and businesses in the community. During the emergency program phase, very limited amounts of coverage are available.

Regular Program

Moving from the emergency program to the regular program requires completion of a more detailed flood insurance study (FIS) by FIMA (not FEMA) and the Army Corps of Engineers, more clearly defining the community's flood hazards. Simultaneously, the community, in conjunction with FEMA, is developing and codifying the flood plain ordinances and laws to regulate construction and maintenance in flood zones and flood ways.

After the flood insurance studies are completed and FEMA is satisfied with the locally adopted flood plain management ordinances, the community moves to the regular program. Once the community enters the regular program, the limits presented above become available.

Flood Plain Management in the Regular Program

Flood plain management is the local community's responsibility. Reviewing and updating existing laws are solely the duty of the participating community; FEMA does not take part in this process. However, if the community fails to comply with its own flood plain management requirements, FEMA may place the community on probation for 1 year.

During that year, every flood policy in that community has a $50 surcharge tacked on to the current premium: to help finance the increased risk the community is presenting and as a political move to encourage policy holders to call the community officials to push for resolution of the problems and end the probation.

The community is no longer considered a participating community as they are not working with FEMA to mitigate losses. If deficiencies are not corrected within that year, the community is suspended, and no NFIP-backed flood policies can be written or renewed.

Policy Terms and Conditions Unique to Flood Coverage

Terms and conditions peculiar to NFIP policies have evolved, changed, and been added since the plan's formation in 1968. Many of these changes have been the result of inflation (such as increasing limits), some the result of actual problems, and still others the product of anecdotal evidence (such as the waiting period change). Some of these provisions are highlighted in the following paragraphs. These are unique requirements and limitations that agents must understand and explain to their flood clients and potential clients.

Waiting Period

All new NFIP flood policies are subject to a 30-day waiting period (with some exceptions). This mandated waiting period applies to both direct policies and policies written through a

Write Your Own (WYO) carrier. Tolling of the 30-day waiting period begins once the application and the estimated premium are received as follows.

- **From the date of the application** if the application and premium payment are received within 10 days of the date on the application; or if the premium and application are mailed via U.S. Postal Service certified mail within 4 days of the application.

- **From the date of receipt at the NFIP** if the application and payment are not received within 10 days of the date on the application; or if the premium and signed application are not mailed via certified mail within 4 days of the date on the application.

Note: The waiting period countdown will not begin until the estimated premium is received.

Losses in progress on the effective date are excluded from coverage. A delay in mailing the application and premium could be the difference between a flood loss being covered and being excluded.

Exceptions to the 30-day waiting period for individual or entity coverage are as follows.

- Renewals – No waiting period provided renewal premiums paid.

- Loan closings – effective at the time closing papers are signed (no waiting period).

- Revision or updates to a FIRM – 1-day waiting period.

- Endorsements to reduce coverage – 1-day waiting period.

Thirty-day elimination periods also apply to endorsements requesting an increase in coverage or a decrease in the deductible. Requests for decreases in coverage or increases in deductible are processed immediately upon receipt.

Direct Loss Only

Standard flood insurance policies cover only direct losses suffered by the insured. There is no provision to pay indirect losses. A direct loss is the actual damage to the real and/or personal property resulting from a covered cause of loss. Indirect loss is the increase in expenses or loss of income created by the direct loss.

Excluded are any additional living expenses incurred while the dwelling is being repaired, as well as any loss of income a business suffers due to the inability to occupy and/or operate the business. Any outlay not directly related to repair or replacement of the damaged property is an out-of-pocket indirect expense for the homeowner. Unrealized income resulting from flood damage is a business's out-of-pocket, indirect cost of a flood.

Deductibles

Deductibles in NFIP policies apply separately to each class of property insured. The insured pays two deductibles following a loss: one for the real property and a second for personal property.

Separated deductibles based on type of property insured is contrary to the homeowners' and the commercial property policies' use of a deductible. Deductibles in these common property policies apply to the loss, not the class of property. Thus, the insured is only responsible for one deductible regardless of the class of property damaged or destroyed rather than two as required by the NFIP policy.

Standard NFIP deductibles and rate credits for the various deductible options can be found on FEMA's website. Factors and credits are based on the following.

- The flood zone
- A structure's status as Pre-FIRM or Post-FIRM
- The classification of the structure (residential, other residential, nonresidential)
- The type of property insured: building or contents

Increased Cost of Compliance

Increased Cost of Compliance (ICC) found in Coverage D is mandatory on all three standard flood insurance policy forms in regular program communities. ICC coverage is not available for structures in emergency program communities or for individual units in a residential condominium association.

Communities which have adopted flood plain management requirements within their ordinance or law provisions may require certain structures to be altered or removed following flood damage. Such consequential expense is only available through Coverage D. ICC coverage will pay these additional costs.

- Elevate the structure as required by local code
- "Flood proof" the structure
- Relocate the structure
- Demolish the structure

The $30,000 ICC limit is paid in addition to the amount of direct flood damage. However, FEMA's payment will never exceed the maximum available coverage, even when ICC coverage is added. For example, the insured purchases the maximum amount of dwelling coverage available in the dwelling form ($250,000); if there is a $245,000 direct loss, the maximum coverage available under the ICC extension is $5,000, regardless of the total cost to comply with an ordinance or law. This is why the premiums for ICC coverage decrease after the dwelling limit surpasses $230,000 for residential structures and $480,000 for nonresidential structures.

To be eligible for ICC coverage, the structure must meet one of two requirements (in addition to those previously discussed).

- The structure must be a "repetitive loss structure" for which NFIP has paid a previous qualifying claim in addition to the current damage.
- The structure must sustain "substantial" flood damage ("substantial" is defined in an upcoming section).

Reduction or Reformation of Coverage

Flood policies can be "re-formed" and the limits reduced if the premium paid is not sufficient to cover the amount of coverage requested. Such issues can result for various reasons, including 1) the difference between the Base Flood Elevation (BFE) and the reference point is miscalculated, or 2) the completion of structural changes moving the reference point to a lower level (such as by enclosing the area under an elevated floor in a Flood Zone "A").

If the deficiency is discovered by or reported to FEMA prior to the loss, the insured is given 30 days to pay the difference between the 1-year premium paid and the correct policy-year premium based on actual rating information. However, if the discrepancy is found at the time of the loss, the insured is allowed 60 days to cover the difference in paid and actual premium for the last 2 policy years. Seems generous except for the fact that the insured has no place to live, has to come up with additional premium while also paying for a hotel room, and has to negotiate with one or more insurance carriers (wind and water damage).

Potentially severe penalties apply if the insured does not or cannot pay the additional premium. Insureds unable or unwilling to pay the difference will see the limits on their policy reduced to match the premium paid.

Coverage limit difference resulting from reformation is easily illustrated using a 1-story dwelling in a flood zone "A." For sake of the example, assume a $250,000 limit and standard deductibles, and ignore all policy fees. If the premium is calculated at 2 feet above Base Flood Elevation (BFE), the basic premium for the structure is $355. But if the reference point is actually only 1 foot above BFE, the base premium would be $530.

Although there is only a $175 difference in base premium, there is a huge difference in the amount of coverage that can be purchased. At 1 foot above BFE, the $355 premium can only purchase $45,000 of flood coverage for the subject dwelling, a $205,000 reduction in coverage due to the miscalculation. If this were discovered at the time of the loss, the insured would have 60 days to pay an additional $350. This could easily be done as that is relatively inexpensive, but if the insured cannot come up with it, they are losing a lot of coverage.

The above produces a minor difference in premium, but what is the difference in premium when insureds enclose the area beneath an elevated structure, thereby changing the reference level to some point below BFE? There are several problems created in this case (among them, violation of flood plain management laws, making the structure ineligible for coverage, etc.), but for sake of the discussion, reformation of the coverage is the issue.

This problem is very common among insureds who buy vacation homes on the coast. Some insureds purchase a home and after a couple of years decide to enclose and make use of the wasted space below the house. Doing so drastically changes the reference point; now the structure in the above example may be 5 feet below BFE. The previously paid premium may only purchase $5,000 worth of coverage (just a guess), and the insured would have to pay an additional $2,000 or $3,000 premium to garner the coverage they thought they had (if they can get it at all).

Lesson learned: The agent needs an updated current photo or to conduct an inspection of the house at least bi-annually to confirm there have been no such changes. Such action can lessen the chances of an errors and omissions loss from the "You never told me ..." charges the insured client may lob in the event he suffers a loss.

Unique Flood Policy Definitions

Flood: All three NFIP policies define flood as: A general and temporary condition of partial or complete inundation of two or more acres (general) or two or more properties (at least one of which is the policyholder's property) of normally dry land area (temporary) from one of the following.

- Overflow of inland or tidal waters
- Unusual and rapid accumulation or runoff of surface waters from any source
- Mudflow

Flood also includes the collapse or subsidence of land along the shore of a lake or similar body of water as a result of erosion or undermining caused by waves or currents of water exceeding anticipated cyclical levels that result in a flood as defined above. There are four concepts on which to focus in this definition.

1. The definition states "two or more properties...". It does not state "structures" or who the owner of the second property must be. If the contiguous flood crosses onto another's property, the inundation qualifies as a "flood."

2. The "Southfork Ranch" provision (where the Ewings lived in TV's *Dallas*, before the encroachment of housing developments). Insureds who own a large amount of land may never qualify for coverage without this two-acre provision.

3. Mudflow in the flood policy is not synonymous with mudslide. It means a river of liquid and flowing mud on the surfaces of normally dry land areas.

4. The collapse or subsidence of land does not mean erosion over long periods of time; this is sudden erosion caused by the inundation by flood waters.

Basement: Any area of the building, including any sunken room or sunken portion of a room, having its floor below ground level (sub-grade) on all sides. A very important definition because there is no coverage for any personal property located in a basement, regardless of the flood zone. Overall, there is very limited coverage for property in a basement. Some coverage is extended to property necessary for the operation of the structure and attached to a power source such as electrical equipment (outlets, switches, junction boxes, and circuit breakers), HVAC and AC systems, water heaters, pumps, clothes washers and dryers, and freezers (not walk-in).

Coverage for real property in basements is limited to: drywall for walls and ceilings in a basement to include the cost of labor to nail it, unfinished, un-floated and not taped, to the framing, elevators, dumbwaiters, and related equipment, except for related equipment installed below the Base Flood Elevation after September 30, 1987, nonflammable insulation in a basement, stairways and staircases attached to the building, not separated from it by elevated walkways and footings, foundations, posts, pilings, piers, or other foundation walls and anchorage systems required to support a building.

To be considered a basement, the area must be below ground level on all sides. Walkout basements not requiring a step up to grade are not considered a basement by definition; that is just the first floor and the reference point for flood rating purposes.

Conversely, the building may be above grade but have an area that is dug into the ground making that area below grade and a basement by definition. Coverage for property in such areas is limited as detailed above. Examples may include a sunken living room or a recessed production area.

- **Sunken living rooms** were fashionable in the 1970s and are returning to vogue in some areas of the country. If these areas are below grade even though the rest of the house is above, they are considered basements and none of the property located in them is covered for damage resulting from flood.

- **Recessed production areas** may be necessary due to the weight of the equipment or the process of manufacturing. Such large scale operations may require some excavation to assure the production floor is on solid footing. If the area is below grade on all sides due to this excavation, it is considered a basement; there will be no coverage for the machinery or equipment in such areas.

- *Note:* Sometimes, computer rooms are moved to a basement due to the need for security, segregation, or to avoid damage by sprinkler leakage. None of the computer equipment kept in these areas is covered by the NFIP policy if flood damage occurs.

Elevated Building: A non-basement building with its lowest elevated floor raised above ground level by foundation walls, shear walls, posts, piers, pilings, or columns. Personal property and real property located below the reference point in an elevated structure are subject to the same conditions and limitations as property located in a basement. Additional problems are created if the reference level is altered in an elevated structure.

Pre-FIRM and/or Post FIRM: These terms describe the date construction or substantial improvement was completed compared against the date the initial Flood Insurance Rate Map (FIRM) was effective.

- Structures completed or substantially improved prior to the issuance of the community's first FIRM are considered Pre- FIRM.

- Structures completed or substantially improved after the issuance of the community's first FIRM are considered Post-FIRM.

Rates differ based on a structure's classification as Pre-FIRM or Post-FIRM. Grandfather laws are also affected by Pre- or Post- FIRM designations.

Post-FIRM structures must comply with the floodplain management requirements and the FIRM in effect at the time of construction. Nothing should be done to the structure to alter it in violation of the subject FIRM.

Grandfather Laws: These rules were established for the benefit of policyholders who have either built in compliance with the FIRM in effect at the time of construction, and/or have maintained continuous coverage. Insureds qualifying under Grandfather Laws have the option of using the most favorable rating data, either: 1) the most recent Flood Insurance Rate Map (FIRM), or 2) the rating criteria in effect when the structure was built or coverage was first obtained. The ability to procure coverage based on prior rating criteria is extremely important in at least three situations.

1. The structure is remapped into a Special Flood Hazard Area where it was previously part of a non-special flood hazard area (flood insurance may be required by the mortgagee where it wasn't before).

2. The Base Flood Elevation (used for rating) changes. The difference between the BFE and the reference point may be less, or the reference level may even

move to below the BFE as a result of the remapping, exponentially increasing the cost of flood coverage.

3. The expansion of Coastal Barrier Resource System areas.

Qualifications under Grandfather Laws differ based on the insured's history of flood coverage. Insureds already covered by an NFIP policy need only meet a short list of requirements to qualify for Grandfather status.

- The structure must have been built in compliance with the FIRM in effect at the time of construction.
- Flood coverage must have been continuous.
- No alterations can have been made changing the reference level.

If there has not been previous flood insurance or a prior policy was not renewed, the structure owner can still qualify, but the requirements are a bit more stringent. Rates can be based on the FIRM and Base Flood Elevation in effect when the building was constructed provided all requirements are met.

- Proper documentation is submitted indicating the date of the FIRM (when constructed) and the Zone applied at the time of construction.
- It can be proven through documentation from a community official that the building was constructed in compliance with the map and flood plain management requirements in effect at the time it was built.

- Proof is supplied that the building has not been altered in any way that would have changed the original reference point level.

Two actions of the building owner will negate the ability to qualify for the preferred rates offered by Grandfather Laws.

1. If an elevated building is altered changing the reference level to below the Base Flood Elevation.

2. The building undergoes substantial improvement or suffers substantial damage (both terms defined below).

A campaign of remapping and updating FIRMs is underway due to outdated information on current Flood Insurance Rate Maps. Development, updated flood protection, and even inadequate flood protection are driving the need for this remapping. More insureds may be pulled into Special Flood Hazard Areas. As remapping continues, understanding Grandfather Laws is going to become more important for agents.

Substantial: FEMA defines substantial to mean an amount that exceeds 50 percent of the structure's market value. This applies to "Substantial Improvement" and "Substantial Damage" as follows:

- **Substantial Improvement:** Any reconstruction, rehabilitation, addition, or other improvement to a building, the **cost** of which equals or exceeds 50 percent of the market value of the building before the start of construction of the improvement. Substantial improvement includes buildings that have incurred "substantial damage," regardless of the actual repair work performed. The term does not, however, include either any project for improvement of a building to correct existing state or local code violations or any alteration to a "historic building," provided that the alteration will not preclude the building's continued designation as a "historic building."

- **Substantial Damage:** Damage of any origin whereby the cost of restoring the building to its pre-damaged condition would equal or exceed 50 percent of the market value of the building before the damage occurred.

Market Value is negotiated between and agreed to by a willing buyer and a willing seller. It can fluctuate up and down based on the economy, condition, use, or need, and has little relation to the true cost to rebuild a particular structure. Beyond the fact that market value has no fixed basis, two problems are created when market value is used to calculate substantial improvement: improvements do not have to be structural in nature to increase the market value by 50 percent. The owner may completely remodel and update the kitchen and bathrooms; this could easily increase market value by at least 50 percent; and who knows what the market value was before the improvements were completed? Unless an analysis was completed by a licensed appraiser before improvements began, this is just a FEMA-induced guess.

CBRA Zones and Otherwise Protected Areas (OPAs)

Rapid development in coastal areas, on barrier islands, and near habitat-rich wetland areas prompted the Federal government to pass the Coastal Barrier Resources Act of 1982 (CBRA). This was a legislative effort to minimize loss to human life, eliminate wasteful Federal expenditures, and prevent damage to fish, wildlife, and natural resources in protected areas by discouraging further development. Coastal Barrier Resource System (CBRS) units were delineated by Congress, with help from agencies within the Department of the Interior, creating areas of land subject to passive Federal protection.

Congress expanded on the CBRS units with the adoption of the Coastal Barrier Improvement Act of 1990 (CBIA). This act added CBRS units not part of the original act and created additional zones known as "Otherwise Protected Areas" (OPAs).

Otherwise Protected Area (OPA) boundaries generally follow Federal, state, or local park boundaries and include land used for recreation or conservation. However, OPAs are not always restricted to these properties. Congress intentionally incorporated undeveloped land located contiguous to defined park land into OPAs. Individuals and private entities own some of this undeveloped land.

These two acts combine to remove 3.1 million acres of land (1.3 million CBRS and 1.8 million OPAs) from eligibility for Federal flood protection through the NFIP.

Federal Funds in Protected Areas

Federal spending is strictly limited in CBRS units. Federal monies are available only to fund emergency assistance (not the same as disaster assistance), military activities necessary for national security, exploration for and removal of energy resources and the maintenance of existing Federal navigation channels. Individuals and entities within a CBRS unit cannot receive Federally-backed loans (i.e., VA, FHA, Fannie Mae or Freddie Mac loans) nor is Federal flood insurance available.

Only one restriction on Federal money applies in Otherwise Protected Areas. The only limitation on Federal funding in an OPA is Federal flood insurance. Structures located in an OPA cannot purchase flood coverage through the National Flood Insurance Program (NFIP).

A 2002 U.S. Fish and Wildlife Service study estimates that from 1983 through 2010 Federal fund restrictions mandated by these Acts will have resulted in $1.3 billion in savings to taxpayers. Restrictions on Federal spending for roads, wastewater systems, potable water supply, disaster relief, and flood insurance in these restricted areas combine to create this savings.

Grandfather Laws in CBRS and OPAs

Structures existing prior to the adoption of these Acts garner grandfather status and remain eligible for Federal flood coverage provided they were built or substantially improved on or before specified dates and have not suffered substantial damage. Grandfather status is granted as follows.

- To any structure in a CBRS unit created by the CBRA of 1982 built or substantially improved on or before October 1, 1983.
- To any structure in a CBRS unit added by the CBIA of 1990 built or substantially improved on or before November 1, 1990.
- To any structure in an OPA built or substantially improved on or before November 16, 1991.

Grandfathered buildings suffering substantial damage, from any hazard (fire, wind, or flood), or substantially improved after the above dates lose eligibility under the Grandfather Laws and no longer qualify for flood coverage through the NFIP. (Substantial damage and substantial improvement were defined above.)

Passive Federal Protection

Restrictions on the availability of Federal money for loans or Federal flood coverage in these protected areas do not preclude the use of free market loans or open market flood insurance. Further, these laws do not disallow building and development in these areas; they just don't allow the use of Federal dollars to finance, insure, build roads to, or supply potable water to such development.

Owners are allowed to develop their property as they desire (subject to building codes and laws) but without any Federal money. The government did not take away property rights, just the availability of Federal funds, thus the term "Passive Federal Protection."

Determination of Coverage Eligibility

Only the U.S. Fish and Wildlife Service can officially determine if a property is located in a CBRS unit or an OPA. Although these zones are indicated on applicable Flood Insurance Rate Maps (FIRMs), boundary lines on older FIRMs are only approximations and can be off by as much as 100 yards (affecting as many as three houses). No local surveyor, building inspector, or other town official has the authority to make an official determination.

Standard flood insurance policies require that if any part of a structure is in a Special Flood Hazard Area (SFHA), the entire building must be rated in the higher risk zone as per the prior discussion. However, this rule does not necessarily apply in CBRS units or OPAs. If a building is dissected by a CBRS or OPA boundary line, provisions in the law may allow the property to remain eligible for Federal flood coverage. Decisions are made on a case-by-case basis depending on the specific details and history of the property in question.

Additions made to a structure after an eligibility ruling has been made can be problematic. Expansion on the seaward side of the dissecting boundary line could jeopardize the structure's continued eligibility. However, additions on the leeward side should not result in any coverage issues (provided there is no change in the reference level).

Locations of CBRA Zones and OPAs

Twenty-one states, Puerto Rico and the Virgin Islands are home to CBRS units or OPAs. States containing these units are: Alabama, Connecticut, Delaware, Florida, Georgia, Louisiana, Maine, Maryland, Massachusetts, Michigan, Minnesota, Mississippi, New Jersey, New York, North Carolina, Ohio, Rhode Island, South Carolina, Texas, Virginia, and Wisconsin.

The Coastal Barrier Resources Reauthorization Act was last reauthorized in 2005. Changes to these boundary lines and locations can only be made by an act of Congress. The most recent changes were made in 2016.

Key Questions

- Is the structure located in an NFIP-participating community?
- Is the structure Pre-FIRM or Post-FIRM?
- In what flood zone is the structure located? Do flood zones
  change near the structure (i.e., from "X" to "A")?
- Is the dwelling located in a Special Flood Hazard Area?
- Does the structure have a "basement" as defined in the policy?
- If located in a Zone "V": Is the structure elevated on piers, posts, pilings, etc.?

- If located in a Zone "A": Do solid foundation perimeter walls have proper engineered openings (1 sq. inch per 1 sq. foot of enclosed space)?
- Is the structure located in a CBRA zone or OPA?
- When was the last elevation certificate completed?
- What is the height above Base Flood Elevation (BFE)?
- Have there been any additions to the structure since the last elevation certificate was completed?
- When was the last photo provided?
- Have there been any improvements or betterments to the structure (external additions, internal upgrades, etc.)? If "yes," what were the improvements and what was the cost of improvements?
- Has the structure been damaged by any cause of loss (fire, wind, flood, etc.)?
- Has the insured previously carried flood coverage on the structure? When?
- Is coverage needed for a loan closing? (If not, explain waiting period.)
- Has the community been remapped recently?

Chapter 15

How to Write Coverage for Condominium Associations and Unit Owners

Completing the condominium insurance picture necessitates jigsaw puzzle tenacity. Quite a few pieces must be snapped together to assure the proper insurance picture is presented. Any missing information can leave a gaping hole in either the association's or unit owner's coverage picture. Regardless of the client's status as the association or individual unit owner, the puzzle cannot be completed until the agent can connect the answers to two questions.

1. Who is responsible for insuring which property?
2. What is the value of the insured property?

Who Insures Which Property?

Associational responsibility is divided into three levels: "Original specifications," "all-in," and "bare walls." Each level of responsibility presented above, and definition presented in this chapter is from the association's perspective, delineating which part of the real property it, the association, is responsible for insuring. Property not insured by the association must be protected by the unit owner's insurance policy.

To fully understand the three levels of associational responsibility first requires the four categories of condominium real property be specifically described. The four categories are: common elements, limited common elements, unit property, and unit improvements and betterments.

Each category of condominium real property is generally defined in one of two places: the association's covenants, conditions, and restrictions (CCRs); or the statutes of the state in which the association is located. If not defined in one of these places, the agent can and probably should apply the definitions provided in the most current edition of the Uniform Common Interest Ownership Act.

Condominium Real Property Definitions

Common elements are owned by and benefit, to some extent, all members of the association. Land, parking lots, and the building's structural foundations and load-bearing walls are examples of common elements. Also included in this definition are club houses, pool houses, pools, fences, gates, playground equipment, tennis courts, and other property owned by and allocated to all unit owners. Not all property categorized as a common element is insurable in standard property policies (i.e., land), but most can be scheduled.

Limited common elements are beneficial to more than one but fewer than all unit owners. Common hallways or corridors providing access to several units, walls and columns containing electrical wiring or sprinkler piping serving or protecting multiple units, or a plenum enclosure providing heating and cooling to multiple units are examples. Doorsteps, stoops, decks, porches, balconies, patios, exterior doors and windows, or other fixtures designed to serve a single unit but located outside the unit's boundaries are often categorized as limited common elements because the appearance and safety of these fixtures directly affects multiple unit owners although connected to just one unit.

Unit property is defined by the association declarations or statute and is limited to and benefits only the unit owner. The inside of the exterior walls, interior partition walls, counter tops, cabinetry, plumbing fixtures, appliances, and any other real property confined to the unit are examples. The definition of unit property can vary widely with no universal designation.

Unit Improvements and betterments, like unit property, benefit none but the unit owner. The three previous definitions of associational responsibility classifications require improvements and betterments be classed separately— excluding improvements and betterments from the definition of covered property under the association's policy. A "unit improvements and betterment" is created by the unit owner's engagement in any activity or improvement that increases the value of the real property within an individual unit, such as updating the flooring to hardwood from carpet or other such improvements.

Levels of Associational Responsibility Explained

"Original specification" requirements, known as "single entity coverage," make the association responsible for the common elements, limited common elements, and unit property. Unit improvements and betterments are not the responsibility of the association. Connecting the pieces:

- The association insures the common elements, limited common elements, and unit property.
- Unit owners insure unit improvements and betterments and their personal property within the unit.

A majority of states default to some form of original specification wording as recommended by the Uniform Common Ownership Interest Act.

"All in" ("all inclusive") statutes differ from original specification wording in one major aspect: the association's additional responsibility to insure unit improvements and betterments. In addition to insuring common elements, limited common elements, and unit property, associations are also charged with insuring unit improvements and betterments in "all in" jurisdictions. In other words:

- Associations subject to "all in" wording insure common elements, limited common elements, unit property, and unit improvements and betterments.
- Unit owners insure only personal property within the unit.

Approximately half of the states not applying "original specification" requirements utilize some form of "all inclusive" wording. Only a few of those states apply statutory terminology that could be exclusively interpreted as "all in."

*"**Bare walls**"* wording limits associational insurance responsibility to the common elements and limited common elements. To complete the puzzle:

- The association insures the common elements and the limited common elements.

- Unit owners are tasked with insuring unit property, any unit improvements and betterments, and the owner's personal property within the unit.

At issue in a "bare wall" situation is the definition of "unit." "Unit" does not have a universal or even uniform definition. Unit boundaries, the beginning of the area the association is not responsible for insuring, can be everything from the studs, to the unfinished walls (meaning the paint is insured by the unit owner), to the sub-floor and underside of the ceiling, or any other variation. Dividing responsibility for insuring real property may not be the most advantageous for the association or the unit owner; however, there are several states and individual associations that apply some form of "bare walls" wording.

NFIP – A Special Case

Two standard flood insurance policies (SFIPs) connect in condominium forms of ownership: the Residential

Condominium Building Association Policy (RCBAP) provides coverage for the association and the Dwelling Form is purchased by the individual unit owner to cover personal property. These forms apply as per NFIP standards regardless of any statutory or associational declaration regarding insurance responsibility. (See Chapter 14 for more information on flood policy forms.)

The RCBAP policy form specifically states that coverage is provided for all real property to include real property that is part of the unit. FEMA guidelines further clarify in rule IV. COVERAGE:

A. Property Covered:
"The entire building is covered under one policy, including both the common as well as individually owned building elements within the units, improvements within the units, and contents owned in common. Contents owned by individual unit owners should be insured under an individual unit owner's Dwelling Form."

In essence, the RCBAP is "all in" coverage.

Flood insurance policies do not have to necessarily comply with statute or associational guidelines. When insuring a condominium association or unit owner, agents must be aware of the differences mandated by the NFIP.

Default Setting

Covenants, conditions and restrictions (aka bylaws and declarations) are the primary governing documents of all condominium or unit owner regimes. These documents supersede statute according to the subject statutes themselves. Division of ownership and insurable interest is dictated by these documents. Statutory wording is only the default setting if the bylaws or declarations are silent or are ambiguous regarding the insurance requirements.

In interpreting these documents (or even statutes if necessary) agents should not depend on their own experience or expertise. Attorney opinions should be secured and kept on file for all associations the agency insures or in which they have unit-owner clients. But keep in mind, even attorneys can disagree on specific provisions within the documents.

Exhibit 15.1 at the end of this chapter lists individual state statutes regarding associational level of responsibility. Statute information could not be located for the District of Columbia or Oklahoma.

At What Value? Valuing Association and Unit Owner's Property

Statutes and even associational declarations differ on the valuation method required when placing insurance coverage on the association's property. Actual cash value (ACV), replacement cost (RC), and even market value are mandated options in statute and associational declarations and bylaws.

Most statues require actual cash value as recommended by the Uniform Common Interest Act. In contrast, the Ohio statute requires the association property be insured based on fair market value while other statutes mandate replacement cost. Again, statutes are only the default setting. Insurance limits should be no less than the amount developed when the valuation method required by the association's declarations is applied to the property. However, replacement cost is recommended regardless of the amount required by statute or the covenants, conditions, and restrictions (CCRs).

Defined Values

Three distinctly different property values can be assigned to associational property: replacement cost, actual cash value, and market value. Two are common to insurance, and one generally has no relevance in insurance, until the government or an unknowing attorney gets involved.

Replacement cost (RC) is the cost to replace with new material of like kind and quality on the date of the loss. There is no allowance or penalty for age, depreciation, or condition. The insured must simply insure the property at what it will cost to buy or build it today.

Actual cash value (ACV) is the cost new (replacement cost) minus *physical* depreciation. Physical depreciation results from use and ultimate wear and tear meaning that the insured does not get paid for the "used up" value of the property.

"Physical" is highlighted because there are many different types of depreciation such as depreciation due to obsolescence, accounting depreciation, and economic depreciation. None of these relate to the insurance definition of depreciation, which is physical depreciation due to use.

Market value is negotiated between and agreed to by a willing buyer and a willing seller. It can fluctuate up and down based on the economy, condition, use, or need and has little relation to the true cost to rebuild a particular structure. Normally market value has little relationship to insurance. The rise and fall of the market value does not necessarily change the cost to rebuild a building following a loss.

If the market value is the rule applied in a particular state or association's declarations, the agent must be prepared for and be able to explain this concept regardless of the fact that such value is not normally associated with property insurance values.

Values and Coverage Provided by the Unit-Owners Form (HO 00 06)

Unendorsed, the Unit-Owners Form provides replacement cost coverage on the building (Coverage A) and actual cash value on personal property (Coverage C). Coverage A is limited to a specified amount ($1,000 or $5,000) unless specifically increased by the unit owner. The owner's need to increase Coverage A is a function of the coverage required to be provided by the association based on the level of associational responsibility defined above.

Both Coverage A and Coverage C apply Broad Form Named Perils coverage unless endorsed to cover special causes of loss. Expansion to "open perils" coverage can be accomplished by attaching HO 17 31 to Coverage C and the HO 17 32 to Coverage A.

Coverage C can be transformed from actual cash value to replacement cost with the attachment of the HO 04 90 – **Personal Property Replacement Cost Loss Settlement** endorsement.

Developing Property Insurance Values

Establishing associational and unit owner property values requires knowing who is responsible for insuring which property and which valuation method (RC, ACV, or market value) is being applied.

Cost estimators are effective tools for developing accurate values in most replacement cost and actual cash value settlement scenarios, as are discussions with knowledgeable builders in the area. If market value is the method of valuation, a market analysis by a licensed appraiser may be required to develop the necessary value (it is not recommended that market value ever be used as the insurance value). The accuracy of these calculations varies based on the level of associational responsibility.

Original Specifications: Developing relevant values may be easiest when "single entity" requirements apply as the valuation program and original specification requirements overlap in their result and mandate. Property valuation programs calculate the cost of rebuilding the structure utilizing modern materials of like kind and quality; original specification insurance requirements limit associational responsibility to the cost of replacing original construction materials with modern materials of like kind and quality.

"All-In": All inclusive statutes and associational bylaws increase an association's standard of care. Associations subject to this insurance settlement mandate are forced to closely monitor building and unit values (including value increases created solely by a unit owner) to avoid inadequate insurance and a possible coinsurance penalty that could arise because they (the association) are insuring all real property regardless of location or who installed it. Cost estimators work well in these associations provided the association and the agent are aware of any individual unit owner upgrades.

"Bare Walls": Conflict arises if the unit owner does not have coverage, or enough coverage, to rebuild what is defined as the "unit." The association is only responsible for the common elements and limited common elements. To arrive at the insurance value, a cost estimator has to be completed and the value of each "unit" must somehow be subtracted out of the calculation.

Two questions arise regarding the value of property in a bare walls association.

- Who deciphers the definition of a "unit" allowing the unit owner, the association, and the respective insurance carriers to know who is responsible for insuring what property?

- Who calculates the ultimate amount of coverage needed? There is no available method to produce a verifiable "unit" property value.

Completing the Picture/Key Information

Agents for both the association and the unit owner require the same mass of information to complete the condominium puzzle. To assure that the coverage for the association and the unit owner dovetail seamlessly agents must have the following key information.

- A copy of the association's declarations or covenants, conditions, and restrictions (CCRs).
- A copy of the applicable state statute.
- An official letter documenting the definition of a unit's boundaries detailing who is responsible for insuring which property. Many agents forego this step, depending on their own experience and knowledge to make this determination. This decision could prove detrimental in court.
- A verifiable or signed property valuation calculation. Due to the intricacies of ownership and various combinations of responsibility to which condominium associations and unit owners are subject, getting a written valuation from a specially trained professional or approval from the insured will be beneficial should any question arise. When insuring personal property only, let the insured value his property.

Exhibit 15.1

Individual State Statutes Regarding a Condominium Association's Level of Responsibility

State	Statute
Alabama	35-8A
Alaska	AS 34.08
Arizona	33
Arkansas	18.13
California	1371
Colorado	38-33
Connecticut	47-828
Delaware	25.22
Florida	718.111
Georgia	44.3.3
Hawaii	514B
Idaho	55.15
Illinois	765.605
Indiana	32.25
Iowa	499B
Kansas	58.31
Kentucky	381
Louisiana	RS9
Maine	33.10
Maryland	RP 11
Massachusetts	II-183A
Michigan	Act 59

Minnesota	515
Mississippi	9.89
Missouri	29.448
Montana	70.23
Nebraska	76
Nevada	116-1
New Hampshire	Title XXXI 356B
New Jersey	46.8B
New Mexico	47-7C
New York	9B-339
North Carolina	47C-2-102
North Dakota	47-04
Ohio	5311
Oregon	Ch. 100
Pennsylvania	3312
Rhode Island	34-36
South Carolina	27-31
South Dakota	
Tennessee	66-27
Texas	Prop. Title 7.82
Utah	57.8
Vermont	27-15
Virginia	55-4.2-79
Washington	64-34
West Virginia	36A-8
Wisconsin	Ch. 703
Wyoming	34-20

Chapter 16

Understanding Covered Auto Symbols in the Business Auto Policy

ISO's Business Auto Coverage (BAC) Form (CA 00 01) protects the named insured ("you") against the financial consequences of its legal liability for bodily injury or property damage not excluded by the policy and arising out of the ownership, maintenance or use of a covered auto. This makes the covered auto symbols the key to the Business Auto Coverage Form. Each symbol grants insured auto status to a different class of vehicle.

Nine predefined coverage symbols (1 – 9) trigger protection to a progressively narrowing definition of insured vehicles. For example, Symbol 1 extends protection to "Any Auto," while Symbol 7 provides coverage for only "Specifically Described Autos." The ability to add "special instruction" symbols (10, 11, etc) exist beyond the nine specifically defined symbols. A relatively recent edition to the list of covered auto symbols is Symbol 19, which extends coverage for "mobile equipment" that, for whatever reason, must be registered for use on public roads.

The agents' goal is (or should be) to use the broadest symbol allowed to extend coverage to the greatest number of vehicle classes (owned, nonowned, hired or borrowed).

Symbol 1 – Any Auto

"Any," as provided in Symbol 1, contains no limitations; it means exactly what it says. Regardless of the auto's status as owned, nonowned, hired, borrowed, or other status, it is covered. The only limitations on an "Any Auto" auto are the policy exclusions. Essentially, if the named insured (the "you") or "automatic insured" (subject to five exceptions) are held legally liable for injury arising out of the ownership, maintenance, or non-excluded use of an auto, the BAC provides coverage.

Symbol 1 is almost exclusively a liability coverage symbol. It is unlikely underwriters will allow its use with any other auto policy coverage type (e.g., medical payments, uninsured and underinsured motorists (UM/UIM), or physical damage).

Due to the breadth of insured vehicle status granted by Symbol 1 (owned, nonowned, and hired), it should be used to trigger liability coverage whenever possible. However, use of Symbol 1 may not always be appropriate. Specific inappropriate Symbol 1 usage generally flows from the unique risk characteristics of a particular insured.

Coverage to Equal Symbol 1

Beyond the rare cases of inappropriate Symbol 1 usage, there are occasions when underwriters simply will not entertain extending liability protection to Any Auto. Such refusal might be class-based or due simply to the carrier's underwriting philosophy not to provide Symbol 1.

Accomplishing the goal of providing the broadest definition of insured vehicle without the ability to use Symbol 1 requires a combination of three covered auto symbols: 2 (Owned Autos Only), 8 (Hired Autos), and 9 (Nonowned Autos). Using Symbols 2, 8, and 9 appear to cover the full range of insured vehicle definitions; but do they? Does 2+8+9=1?

Judging the effectiveness of this option's ability to accomplish the goal, each covered auto symbol requires review.

Descriptions of Symbols 2, 8 and 9

Each symbol definition contains clues as to this combination's ability to meet the breadth of covered vehicle definition offered by Symbol 1. Following are the applicable definitions found in ISO's Business Auto Coverage Form.

- *Symbol "2" (Owned "Autos" Only): Only those "autos" you own (and for Liability Coverage any "trailers" you don't own while attached to power units you own). This includes those "autos" you acquire ownership of after the policy begins.*

- *Symbol "8" (Hired "Autos" Only): Only those "autos" you lease, hire, rent or borrow. This does not include any "auto" you lease, hire, rent, or borrow from any of your "employees", partners (if you are a partnership), members (if you are a limited liability company) or members of their households.*

- *Symbol "9" (Nonowned "Autos" Only): Only those "autos" you do not own, lease, hire, rent or*

213

*borrow that are used in connection with your business. This includes "autos" owned by your "employees", partners (if you are a partnership), members (if you are a limited liability company), or members of their households but only while used in your business or your personal affairs. (Emphasis added. **Note**: Essentially, Symbol 9 extends vicarious liability protection to the named insured (the "you") for bodily injury or property damage suffered by a third party caused by someone operating a covered vehicle on the named insured's behalf or benefit.)*

Two important terms must be considered when comparing the breadth of inclusion offered by the amalgamation of these three symbols compared to Symbol 1: "You" (the named insured) and "covered auto" (as defined by each symbol above).

Why "You" Matters

Liability insurance forms always extend the greatest amount of protection to the policy's "You" (also known as the named insured); the BAC is no exception. The definitions of Symbols 2, 8, and 9 refer to the policy's "You" where Symbol 1 does not. This is the first clue that these two options are not equal in breadth of protection.

Who "you" is differs based on the insured's legal structure as a sole proprietor, partner, limited liability company (LLC), or corporation as follows.

- **Sole Proprietor**: The individually named owner is the policy's "you." So the individual must own, hire, or borrow the vehicle. For nonowned coverage to apply, the owner of the nonowned vehicle must be doing something to further the proprietor's business.

- **Partnerships:** Like sole proprietors, the partners are the "you" of the policy. Essentially the same provisions apply to partnerships as sole proprietors.

- **Limited liability companies (LLCs)**: The LLC is the named insured (subject to some state laws), but the policy treats the members of the LLC like partners.

- **Corporations (any type)**: The corporation is the "you" in the policy making everyone else "employees," including the "owner" of small, privately held corporations and the executive officers of large, possibly publically traded corporation.

These differing assignments of status as a "You" lead to gaps in coverage when Symbols 2, 8 and 9 are used in place of 1. The gaps reside within Symbols 8 and 9.

Symbol 1 – Still the Best

Use of the triune symbol options provide nearly the same breadth of coverage as Symbol 1; but not completely. At least two coverage gaps keep the "Any Auto" option the preferred choice: automobile rental and borrowing an employee's car.

Automobile Rental

Symbol 8 may not provide coverage to the named insured (the "you") or the employee if a car is rented in the employee's name rather than the business name. Symbol 1 would provide coverage to the named insured, but not the employee. However, Symbol 9 might cover this exposure as the vehicle could be considered a nonowned auto. Regardless, both gaps can be filled by attachment of CA 20 54 (Employee Hired Autos) which extends coverage to employees who lease autos in their personal name.

Borrowing an Employee's Car

Symbol 8 specifically states that a car "you" borrow from an employee is not a "hired" vehicle. And Symbol 9 only extends vicarious liability protection to the named insured for the employee's use of their personal vehicle on the named insured's account. Coverage gaps are created when the named insured is a sole proprietor, partner, and possibly an LLC. Since these individuals are considered the "you" and the definition specifically excludes coverage for any "you" that borrows an "auto" from an employee (etc.), there is no coverage under the BAC for bodily injury or property damage caused by the use of that borrowed "auto." Symbol 1 contains no such exclusion; the insured entity would still be protected by the policy.

Vicarious Liability

Symbol 9 extends a certain level of vicarious liability to the named insured for the actions of the owners of a nonowned auto. But the degrees of separation protected by the use of this symbol are not crystal clear.

Protection extended by Symbol 9 is limited to specifically-defined nonowned autos *"used in connection with your business."* There exists no definition in the policy for "connection." Does the insured have to directly benefit from the use of the vehicle for coverage to apply; or is only a casual, indirect connection required?

Without a clear directive regarding the extent of coverage, this produces a possible third gap between the use of Symbol 1 and the three replacement symbols.

Finish Line

If (for whatever reason) Symbol 1 is not available, use Symbols 2, 8 and 9. The combination does not completely provide the same breadth of protection, but it is very close. Using multiple symbols to provide auto protection can be compared to trying to create an "all risk" policy (a bad term) by lengthening the list of covered named perils. The two will never provide the same breadth of protection.

(***Ending Note***: If Symbol 2 is unavailable, try using Symbols 3, 4, 8, and 9. Symbol 3 is Owned Private Passenger Autos Only; and Symbol 4 is Owned Autos Other than Private Passenger. Essentially 3 + 4 = 2.)

The BAC's Remaining Coverage Symbols

As mentioned at the beginning of this chapter, the BAC form specifically defines nine auto symbols. Symbols 1,2,8, and

9 were defined and explored above. Following are brief explanations of the remaining coverage symbols.

- **Symbol 3 (Owned Private Passenger "Autos" Only):** As the title suggests, use of this symbol limits protection to only private passenger autos owned by the insured. If the insured acquires any private passenger autos during the policy period, protection is extended to these vehicles during the remainder of the policy period. Use of this symbol is generally limited to liability coverage.

- **Symbol 4 (Owned "Autos" Other than Private Passenger "Autos" Only):** Like Symbol 3, this symbol extends coverage to owned autos, but this extends coverage to only "other than private passenger autos" such as trucks (light, medium, heavy, and extra-heavy). In addition to the vehicle, protection is extended to any nonowned trailer while attached to a vehicle protected under this symbol. If the insured acquires additional "other than private passenger autos" during the policy period, protection is extended to these vehicles during the remainder of the policy period. Use of this symbol is generally limited to liability coverage.

- **Symbol 5 (Owned "Autos" Subject to No-Fault)**: This symbol is used when a vehicle is licensed and principally garaged in a state subject to and under "no-fault" (aka Personal Injury Protection (PIP)) statutes. The symbol extends coverage to any autos newly

218

acquired during the policy period. As suggested, this symbol is limited to no-fault coverage.

- **Symbol 6 (Owned "Autos" Subject to Compulsory Uninsured Motorists Laws)**: This symbol is used when a vehicle is licensed and principally garaged in a state subject to and under uninsured motorist statutes. In these states, the insured cannot reject uninsured motorist coverage. Extends coverage to any autos newly acquired during the policy period. As suggested, this symbol is limited to uninsured motorist coverage.

- **Symbol 7 (Specifically Described "Autos")**: Use of this symbol limits coverage to only those autos specifically listed (scheduled) in the policy. If the auto is not scheduled, there is no coverage. Newly acquired autos are subject to specific restrictions and only a short period of automatic coverage. However, to gain the 30 days of automatic protection granted, the insurance carrier must already insure all the insured's vehicles on the same policy or the new vehicle must be a replacement for an existing auto. If the insurance carrier does not insure all the vehicles on the same policy, and the new vehicle is in addition to the current schedule, there is no automatic coverage on the vehicle, and it is not covered until the insurer is notified of its existence. Symbol 7 is usually limited to physical damage protection, but it can be used to signify liability, uninsured/underinsured motorists, or physical damage.

Key Questions

- Is Symbol 1 available for liability coverage? Is it being used?
- If Symbol 1 is not available, why not?
- Are Symbols 2, 8 and 9 available for liability?
- If using 2, 8 and 9, have the potential gaps been discussed with the insured?
- Are all the insured's vehicles insured on one policy? If not, pay attention to and explain the gap presented by Symbol 7.

Chapter 17

Four Commercial Auto Endorsements Every Insured Should Consider

ISO lists more than 100 endorsements available for use with the Business Auto Coverage Form (BAC) (total numbers vary by state). Out of that heap of policy-altering endorsements, most designed to meet the needs of a specific class of insured or specific state's laws, are at least four that every insured should consider.

Regardless of the industry or state of operation, the following four endorsements alter the availability of coverage for exposures common to most insureds: **Employees as Insureds** (CA 99 33), **Fellow Employee Coverage** (CA 20 55), **Auto Loan/Lease Gap Coverage** (CA 20 71), and **Rental Reimbursement** (CA 99 23). Each is discussed in the following paragraphs.

Employees as Insureds

Coverage granted to the named insured (the policy's "you") in the BAC is initially based on the definition of covered auto as granted by the applicable covered auto symbols. Each symbol grants the insured protection against the financial liability associated with the ownership, maintenance, or use of a specific class of vehicle, owned, nonowned, or hired.

When Symbols 1, 8 or 9 are used, the named insured is financially protected for its vicarious liability arising out of the use of a hired or nonowned auto. This includes protection for the named insured's vicarious liability that can arise from an employee's use of their personal vehicle on the behalf of and for the benefit of the named insured.

Assume, for example, the office manager uses his personal car to make daily trips to the post office, bank, and other places for the benefit of the named insured. Since the named insured is benefiting from the activities of the office manager, it is exposed to vicarious liability for the negligent actions of the office manager. Should the office manager be involved in a serious crash on the way to the bank, the named insured could be held vicariously liable for any injury or damage suffered by a third party.

If the appropriate covered auto symbol(s) is/are used, the named insured's BAC responds, on an excess basis, to protect it for any vicarious liability that may arise from the accident. However, the unaltered BAC will not extend to protect the employee for his liability when using his personal auto for the benefit of the named insured.

In fact, the employee's Personal Auto Policy (PAP) responds first to protect the employee and the company for which he works. The named insured's BAC, by application of the "Other Insurance" provision, actually applies as excess over the at-fault employee's PAP, but, again, only for the benefit of the named insured, not the employee.

To add further insult, the named insured's BAC carrier may even be able to subrogate against the employee to recover any money it pays out on behalf of the named insured because of the employee's negligence. Since the unaltered BAC specifically excludes the employee from insured status while driving his own vehicle, even on company business, the ability to subrogate is retained. Whether the insurer will or can carry through on this opportunity is based on the totality of the surrounding circumstances.

The **Employees as Insureds** (CA 99 33) endorsement closes these gaps and seeming inequities by altering the definition of "Who is an Insured" to include an employee while using an auto the named insured ("you) does not own, hire, or borrow while it is being used on the named insured's behalf. This extends insured status to the employee while using his personal vehicle on company business.

But even with the **Employees as Insureds** endorsement, the employee's PAP remains the primary protection. However, if the total of bodily injury and property damage exceeds the employee's PAP limits, the BAC with the CA 99 33 attached will respond as excess on behalf of both the named insured and the employee. Plus, as an insured, the BAC insurer cannot subrogate against the employee (unless a policy provision is violated, such as intentionally hitting the other person(s)).

Fellow Employee Coverage

Exclusion 5. in the Business Auto Coverage Form in part reads:

"Fellow Employee

Bodily injury to:

a) Any fellow employee of the insured arising out of and in the course of the fellow employee's employment or while performing duties related to the conduct of your business."

In essence, if one employee, through the use of a vehicle, injures a fellow employee on the job, there is no coverage extended from the BAC to protect the at-fault employee.

Combining exclusion 5 with exclusions 3 (Workers' Compensation) and 4 (Employee Indemnification and Employer's Liability) effectively removes any protection available under the BAC for an auto-related injury an employee might suffer in the course of employment (depending on who is classified as an employee based on entity type and law). Work-related injuries are to be covered elsewhere. The employer has the opportunity to purchase workers' compensation to protect it from these exclusions, but an employee has no such commercial insurance option, only a personal insurance option they may not recognize is needed.

Employees who unintentionally cause an auto-related injury to a fellow employee may be left with no insurance protection should the fellow employee file suit. There are three examples of possible fellow-employee gaps.

- The employee driving a company-owned vehicle is negligent in his operation of the vehicle and is involved in an accident causing bodily injury to a co-employee riding with him (depending on the provisions of the business use exclusions and the meaning of furnished for regular use exclusion in the relevant PAP).

- The at-fault employee injures a fellow employee while using a company-owned vehicle assigned to the at-fault employee (a company car). The at-fault employee does not have the proper endorsement on his PAP **(Extended Non- owned Auto)** and is sued by the injured employee.

- During a business trip, the at-fault employee rents a car in the name of his employer to travel to various appointments. He and a fellow-employee are injured in an at-fault accident and the fellow employee sues the driver.

Yes, these are all work-related injuries and the injured fellow employee will be eligible for workers' compensation benefits (provided no policy provisions have been violated). However, this does not preclude the injured employee from suing the at-fault fellow employee. Workers' compensation's benefit as a sole remedy applies only to the employer, not the fellow employee. Some states allow the injured party to also pursue and recover from any fellow employees causing the injury. Such allowance is based on the injury, the benefits received, and the facts of the case. Lacking the correct endorsements on the personal auto policy, the at-fault employee may end up having to pay out-of-pocket for such injuries to a fellow employee.

The **Fellow Employee Coverage (CA 20 55)** endorsement removes the fellow employee exclusion from the BAC allowing the policy to respond on behalf of the at-fault employee following a vehicle-related injury to a fellow employee caused by a covered vehicle. When employers make company-owned vehicles available for employee use or allow employees to rent vehicles to benefit the company, this endorsement should be attached.

Auto Loan/Lease Gap

As the name suggests, this endorsement alters the amount paid under the physical damage section of the BAC to include the difference between the actual cash value (ACV) of the vehicle and the amount remaining on the loan or the amount remaining on the lease. Basically, it helps insureds who are upside down on their loan or lease at the time of the loss.

Obviously, the **Auto Loan/Lease Gap Coverage (CA 20 71)** endorsement is a first-party coverage intended for the benefit of the insured. The coverage allows the insured to satisfy its contract with either the loss payee (lienholder) or lessor.

This endorsement pays the difference between the amount paid by the physical damage coverage and the amount owed, but only when there is a total loss. Payment is limited to the value associated with the specific vehicle. Expenses such as overdue payments, high-mileage and usage penalties, security deposits, add-on costs (i.e., credit life, etc.), and balances from prior loans or leases carried over to the current financing agreement are excluded from coverage.

Vehicle values drop so quickly and the difference between the ACV and the amount owed can be substantial. Consider this endorsement for all insureds with leased or recently-purchased vehicles.

Rental Reimbursement

Insureds do not necessarily need a specific vehicle, they need the use of that or a similar vehicle. The vehicle itself is covered under the physical damage section of the BAC (under Other-Than- Collision or Collision); but the loss of use of that vehicle following a first-party comprehensive or collision loss is not covered by the unendorsed BAC.

When the insured suffers a first-party loss of a covered vehicle, he also loses the use of that vehicle while it is being repaired; a replacement must be procured. **Rental Reimbursement Coverage (CA 99 23)** provides some of the necessary reimbursement to rent a replacement vehicle. This coverage is designed, as the name suggests, to reimburse the insured for the cost to rent a replacement vehicle while a covered vehicle is being repaired following a covered loss. The policy is subject to three maximums: a maximum per day limit; a maximum number of days; and a maximum total per loss, per vehicle. Further, the policy contains a 24-hour "after the loss" time deductible.

Coverage limits should be based on the type of vehicles being replaced. Private passenger autos may easily be attainable for $30 per day, depending on the size of vehicle rented. However, renting a replacement dump truck or other large work vehicle may run as high as $500 or $600 per day. The agent should be familiar with the rental market in the insured's area when selecting limits as the policy limits payment to the lesser of the actual rental cost or the limit purchased.

One last important provision of which the agent needs to be aware: there is no coverage extended from this form if the insured has a spare or reserve auto available for use. The policy pays only when the insured needs a replacement vehicle, not just because the covered vehicle is not available for use due to a covered cause of loss.

Insureds rarely have spare vehicles just sitting around waiting to be used. Generally, the vehicle serves a purpose, and the loss of use of that vehicle can result in financial harm beyond the cost of rent (loss of sales opportunities, the inability to fulfill a contract, etc.). The **Rental Reimbursement Coverage** endorsement finances part of the cost to regain the use of a missing vehicle by replacing it with another for a short period.

Appendix A

Insurer is 'Torturing' Policy Using Pollution Exclusion to Deny Death Claim

U.S. District Judge Lee Rosenthal in Houston was called upon in 2008 to rule on whether Great American Insurance Co. acted within policy and contract language and in accordance with the required utmost good faith in asserting that it did not owe defense or liability protection in the death of three Houston-area office workers from smoke inhalation. Great American contended, according to the Associated Press, that injury by smoke inhalation is excluded under their Commercial General Liability (CGL) policy's total pollution exclusion.

Friend of the Court (amicus curiae) opinions are generally solicited by both sides of a civil suit and from individuals considered unbiased experts in the filed in question rather than from other attorneys.

Although not asked to provide an amicus curiae in this particular case, I have provided such opinions to courts in the past. If I were asked to write a Friend of the Court brief on this particular case, here is how it would look. (*Note:* This is not a complete brief as it lacks citations, documentation, a copy of the policy form in question, and other supporting definitions.

This is but a framework of how it may look and read.

Disclaimer: This is also not construed to be legal advice.)

'Friend of the Court' Opinion for U.S. District Court, Houston

To: U.S. District Judge Lee Rosenthal

Re: Total Pollution Exclusion Defense Offered by Great American Insurance Co.

Your Honor:

Great American Insurance Co. has put forth a unique yet troublesome assertion regarding the purpose and acceptable use of the total pollution exclusion. In truth, Great American is torturing the policy to get the answer they want in an apparent attempt to avoid payment to the survivors of the three victims of smoke inhalation.

At issue is the breadth of the total pollution exclusion compared to the proximate cause of the injuries in the subject case.

The Absolute/Total Pollution Exclusion

Four total pollution exclusion endorsements are filed by Insurance Services Offices (ISO) for use by insurance carriers. Two provide an exception to the total exclusion and two are supposedly "total"; but even "total" has built-in exceptions.

The four forms in question are:

- CG 21 49 – Total Pollution Exclusion Endorsement
- CG 21 55 – Total Pollution Exclusion with A Hostile Fire Exception
- CG 21 65 – Total Pollution Exclusion with a Building Heating, Cooling and Dehumidifying Equipment Exception and a Hostile Fire Exception
- CG 21 98 – Total Pollution Exclusion Endorsement (this endorsement applies only to products/completed operations.)

Regardless of the form, each shares a common bond with the other three: **proximate cause**. Specifically, each exclusionary endorsement requires there first be a **pollution event** leading to the release of pollutants. The policy wording of each form supports this statement as follows (ISO wording):

2. Exclusions

This insurance does not apply to:

Pollution

(1) "Bodily injury" or "property damage" which would not have occurred in whole or part but for the actual, alleged or threatened discharge, dispersal, seepage, migration, release or escape of "pollutants" at any time.

The key phrase is "would not have occurred...but for..." "But for" is the proximate cause wording at issue in this case. A pollution event would have to be the **proximate cause** for the exclusionary wording to apply. In the subject case, the proximate cause of the deaths is fire *not* the requisite pollution event.

Lacking a pollution event, there is no proximate cause between pollution and the injuries.

Reported Proximate Cause

The event that caused these unfortunate smoke inhalation deaths was the intentional setting of a fire. A fire in no way equates to a pollution event. Fire, defined as oxidation rapid enough to produce a flame or a glow, has a visible, destructive, and, in this case, deadly byproduct – smoke. Fire is the proximate cause of these injuries. Had there been no fire, there would have been no injuries.

Smoke resulting from the release and subsequent dissipation of a pollutant will fit in the intended proximate cause addressed by the subject exclusion. But to equate a release of pollution with smoke of an intentionally set fire is, again, torturing the facts and the policy to arrive at an answer in direct defiance of clear contract language.

Rules of contract applied to insurance policies differ slightly from normal rules of contract. In particular, an insurance contract is a contract of adhesion (the insured takes the contract on a take-it-or-leave-it basis with little or no ability to negotiate wording).

Results of Ruling in Favor of Great American

Allowing this defense to stand would be catastrophic; and this is not hyperbole. If smoke from fire can be considered a pollutant, try to imagine the far-ranging applications of this decision to both property and liability policies. Even though this is a liability case, a decision in favor of Great American could result in the following.

- Homeowners suffering only a small fire may be denied coverage for any damages caused by smoke (and that amount could be greater than the damage caused by the fire).

- Business owners may have to pay the cost to repair machinery and equipment damaged by fire-related smoke out of their own pockets (which are now empty because there has been a business shut down).

- Insurance carriers will be encouraged to attach pollution-related exclusions (property and liability) where they would have not otherwise (judicially taking coverage away with no reduction in premium).

Property and liability insurance coverages and policy holders could unjustly suffer based on the outcome of this case. Much is relying on your decision.

Conclusion

Great American eventually dropped its attempt to apply the total pollution exclusion to deny coverage in this case. Other reasons for denial were put forth having no relation to the pollution exclusion. AT the time of this writing, the outcomes are not known.

Author Biography

Christopher J. Boggs is a self-proclaimed insurance geek with a true passion for the insurance profession and a desire for continual learning.

During his career, Boggs has authored hundreds of insurance and risk management-related articles on a wide range of topics as diverse as Credit Default Swaps, the MCS-90, and enterprise risk management.

Boggs has written and published five insurance and risk management books:

- *"The Insurance Professional's Practical Guide to Workers' Compensation: From History through Audit – Second Edition;"*
- *"Business Income Insurance Demystified: The Simplified Guide to Time Element Coverages – Second Edition;"*
- *"Property and Casualty Insurance Concepts Simplified: The Ultimate 'How to' Insurance Guide for Agents, Brokers, Underwriters and Adjusters;"*
- *"Wow! I Never Knew That! 12 of the Most Misunderstood and Misused P&C Coverages, Concepts and Exclusions;"* and
- *"Insurance, Risk & Risk Management! The Insurance Professional's Guide to Risk Management and Insurance."*

A graduate of Liberty University with a bachelor's degree in Journalism, Boggs has continually pursued career-related education, obtaining nine professional insurance designations: the Chartered Property Casualty Underwriter (**CPCU**), Associate in Risk

Management (**ARM**), Associate in Loss Control Management (**ALCM**), Legal Principles Claims Management (**LPCS**), Accredited Advisor in Insurance (**AAI**), Associate in Premium Auditing (**APA**), Certified Workers' Compensation Advisor (**CWCA**), Construction Risk and Insurance Specialist (**CRIS**) and the Associate in General Insurance (**AINS**) designations.

Made in the USA
Las Vegas, NV
16 January 2021